BEST of Knit Picks

ACCESSORIES

Photography by John Cranford & Amy Cave

Printed in the United States of America

First Printing, 2019

ISBN 978-1-62767-251-1

Versa Press, Inc.
800-447-7829

www.versapress.com

CONTENTS

ANDEAN CHULLO HAT

by Kerin Dimeler-Laurence

FINISHED MEASUREMENTS
20-21" head circumference, to fit Adult M

YARN
Knit Picks Palette™ (fingering weight, 100% Peruvian Highland Wool; 231 yards/50g): 1 ball each of nine colors (see chart pages for two colorways)

NEEDLES
US 3 (3.25mm) DPNs or two 24" circular needles for two circulars technique or 32" or longer circular needles for Magic Loop technique, or size to obtain gauge
US 2.5 (3mm) extra needles (any kind)

NOTIONS
Yarn Needle
Stitch Markers
Stitch Holder or Scrap Yarn

GAUGE
32 sts and 40 rows = 4" in stranded Stockinette Stitch worked flat and in the round, blocked

For pattern support, contact customerservice@knitpicks.com

Andean Chullo Hat

Notes:

Andean knitting is known for its brightly-colored stranded designs. Geometric patterns as well as depictions of common things, like farm animals, are the main motifs seen in this region. Designs are often in a solid color over a shifting-color background. Knitting and textile creation are as ubiquitous in Andean society as coffee is to Americans. This cap is inspired by the Andean Chullo (pronounced *tchoo-yo*), which is a traditional garment knit by Andean men, women, and children.

This is a "choose-your-own-adventure" style design; simply plug in the charted design of your choice when the pattern calls for it to make your own unique hat. You can make more than one hat from the yarn requirements by rearranging the colors! Simply cross out and rename the colors as you'd like—but be sure to follow the charts accordingly.

This hat is knit from the earflaps up, with applied I-Cord and tassels to finish. All patterns are worked in stranded Stockinette Stitch.

The earflap charts are worked flat; read RS rows (odd numbers) from right to left, and WS rows (even numbers) from left to right. The remainder of the charts are worked in the round; read all rows from right to left as RS rows.

Applied I-Cord

*K2, Sl1 K-wise. PU and K 1 st from edge of hat. (4 sts on RH needle.) Use LH needle tip to pass Sl st over last knit st. (3 sts on RH needle.) Sl these 3 sts back onto LH needle, P-wise. Tug on working yarn to tighten up sts. Rep from *.

DIRECTIONS

Earflaps

Pick an Earflap chart and make one of each Left and Right design. Be sure to wrap colors around each other, as in intarsia, where the solid color border and the pattern meet.

CO 4 sts in the color used on Row 1 and purl one row.
Work from chart; incs are included and should be knit in the color in which they appear. After last row (WS) break yarn with 6" tails and place live sts on st holder or spare needles.
Make second earflap in the same manner, working from opposite chart. Place on st holder or scrap yarn.

With C1 and using the Cabled Cast On, CO 16 sts. Turn work, hold Left Earflap with RS facing and, holding CO sts in right hand, cont row by knitting across earflap sts. Turn work and CO 64 sts. Turn again and, with RS facing, attach Right Earflap in same manner as Left. Turn work and CO 16 sts. 160 sts total. PM and join to work in the rnd.
Knit one rnd with C1.

Body

Choose any Small Pattern you wish to knit in each of the four Small Pattern bands (see Patterning Diagram for chart placement). Work each chart you choose. You may rep one chart in all four sections, use two of the charts twice, or use different charts for each of the four sections—it's up to you! Work two rnds of C1 between each charted section, the gray lines in the diagram.
After completing two Small Patterns, one Main Pattern, and two more Small Patterns, work two rnds in C1.

Crown

Work all rows of chosen Crown Chart; rep each chart row ten times around, working decs as they appear. 10 sts.
Next Rnd: K2tog around. 5 sts.
Next Rnd: K2tog, K3. 4 sts.
Switch to a CC of your choice and work in 4-st I-Cord for 3".
Break yarn, leaving an 8" tail. BO by passing tail through live sts and pulling tight.

I-Cord Border

With spare DPN and a color of your choice, CO 4 sts.
Work in 4-st I-Cord for 3".
Inc 2 sts into the next rnd. 6 sts.
In the next rnd, the I-Cord will be split into two applied I-Cords that run along the edge of the hat.
K2, Sl1, place next 3 sts on scrap yarn.
Holding hat with RS facing and starting at CO point of one earflap, begin working Applied I-Cord. Work to point of opposite earflap; leave live sts on spare DPN or scrap yarn.
Place sts from scrap yarn on first side onto needle, attach yarn, and work Applied I-Cord around other side, to other held I-Cord end at point of earflap.
Place all 6 sts on one needle and work one rnd in 6-st I-Cord.
On next rnd, dec 2 sts. 4 sts.
Cont in I-Cord for 3".
Break yarn, leaving an 8" tail. BO by passing tail through live sts and pulling tight.

Tassels

Make three yarn tassels using whatever colors you like: a solid, three different colors, or all of the colors combined. The tassels should be approx 3-4" long; use approx 40 strands of yarn per tassel.

Finishing

Attach tassels to ends of each I-Cord. Use tail from top knot of tassel to tie and graft tassel to I-Cord. Pass I-Cord tail through tassel with a yarn needle, and tie again around center of tassel. Trim tassels to even out ends.

Weave in ends; it is only necessary to weave in CO and BO ends and those that would be bothersome or show on the right side. The yarn ends inside hat can be carefully knotted together and cut to approx 0.5". Be sure not to pull on ends while knotting so as not to disturb pattern. Wash and block.

Patterning Diagram

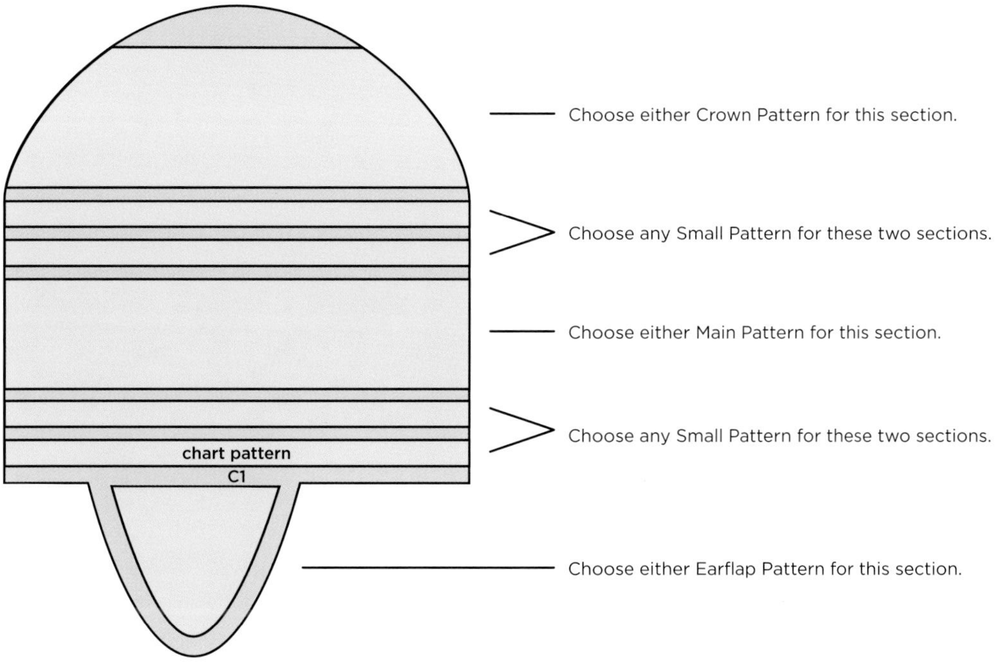

I-Cord Diagram

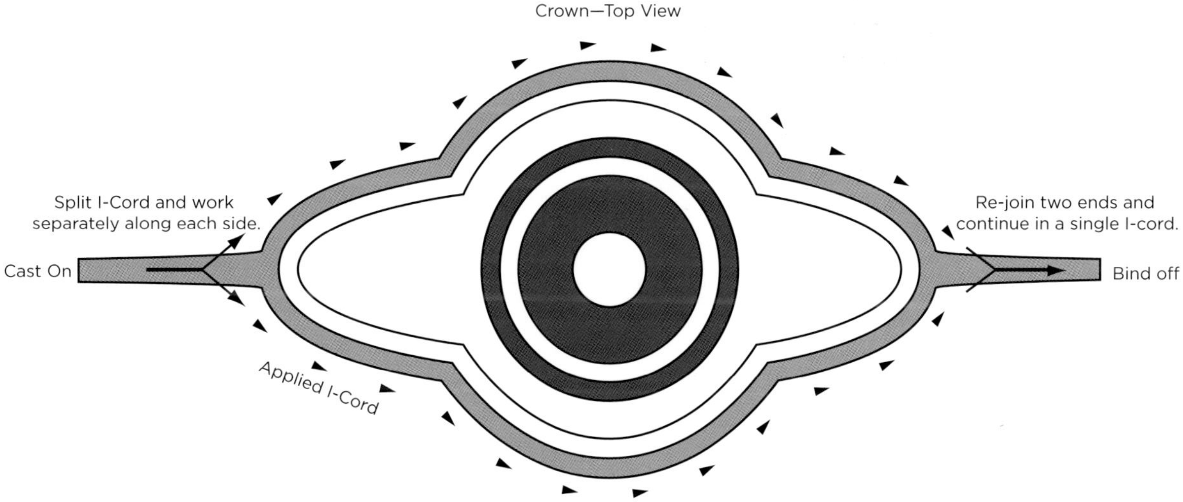

LEGEND: MOUNTAIN PASS COLORWAY

- Shire Heather (C1)
- Shoal
- Lichen
- Tidepool Heather
- Serpentine
- Masala
- Marble Heather
- Mist
- Pimento
- **No Stitch**
  Placeholder—no stitch made
- **K**
  RS: Knit stitch
  WS: Purl stitch
- **M1R** (MR)
  Make 1 right-leaning stitch
- **M1L** (ML)
  Make 1 left-leaning stitch
- **K2tog** (/)
  Knit 2 stitches together as one stitch
- **SSK** (\)
  Slip, slip, knit slipped stitches together

Earflaps—Alpaca—Left

Earflaps—Alpaca—Right

Earflaps—Ripples—Left

Earflaps—Ripples—Right

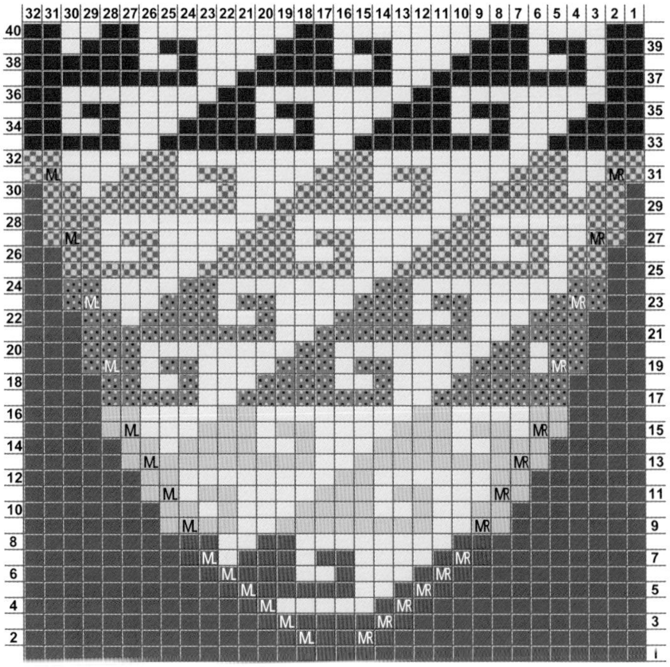

Crown—Chain

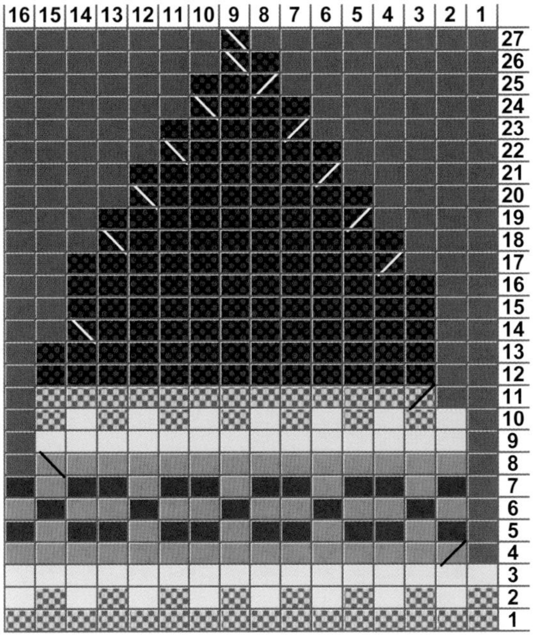

Crown—Coins

Main Pattern—Alpaca

Rep ten times around

Main Pattern—Ripples

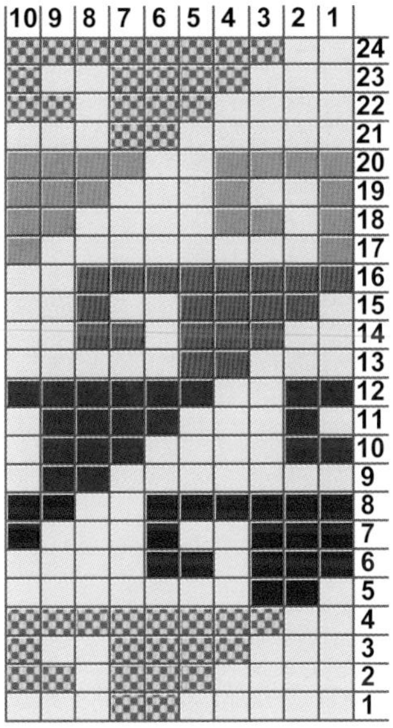

Rep 16 times around

Small Pattern—Dots

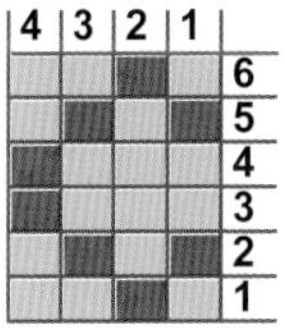

Small Pattern—Flourish

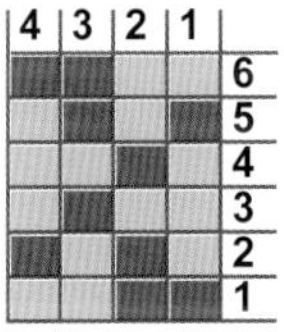

Small Pattern—Little Alpacas

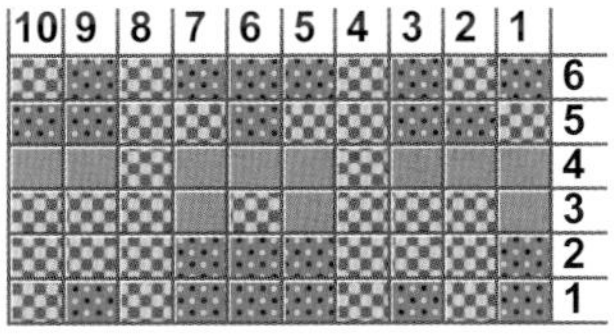

Small Pattern—Spirals

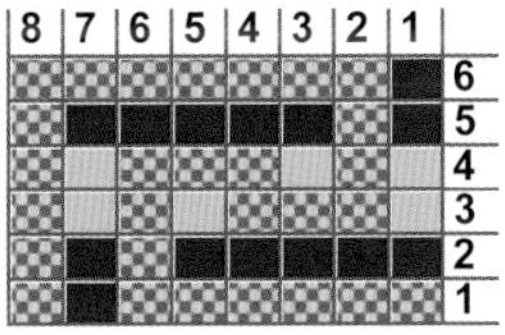

Small Pattern—Tilting Bricks

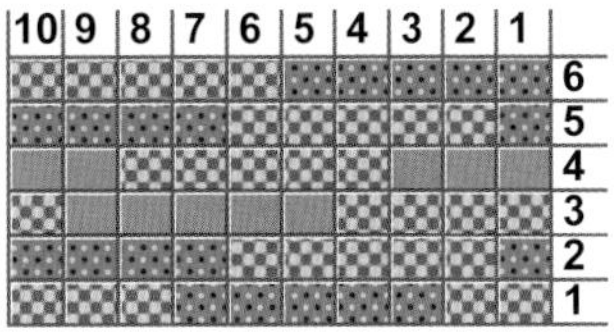

Small Pattern—Little Wave

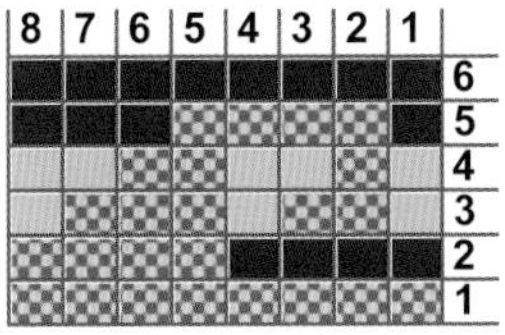

MOUNTAIN PASS COLORWAY

1 ball each:

Shire Heather 26039 (C1)
Shoal 26054
Lichen 26047
Tidepool Heather 24007
Serpentine 25100
Masala 24248
Marble Heather 24244
Mist 23733
Pimento 24246

LEGEND: MOUNTAIN SKY COLORWAY

- Silver (C1)
- Delta
- Sky
- Cyan
- Ash
- Asphalt Heather
- Black
- White
- Marble Heather
- **No Stitch** Placeholder—no stitch made
- **K** RS: Knit stitch WS: Purl stitch
- **M1R** Make 1 right-leaning stitch
- **M1L** Make 1 left-leaning stitch
- **K2tog** Knit 2 stitches together as one stitch
- **SSK** Slip, slip, knit slipped stitches together

Earflaps—Alpaca—Left

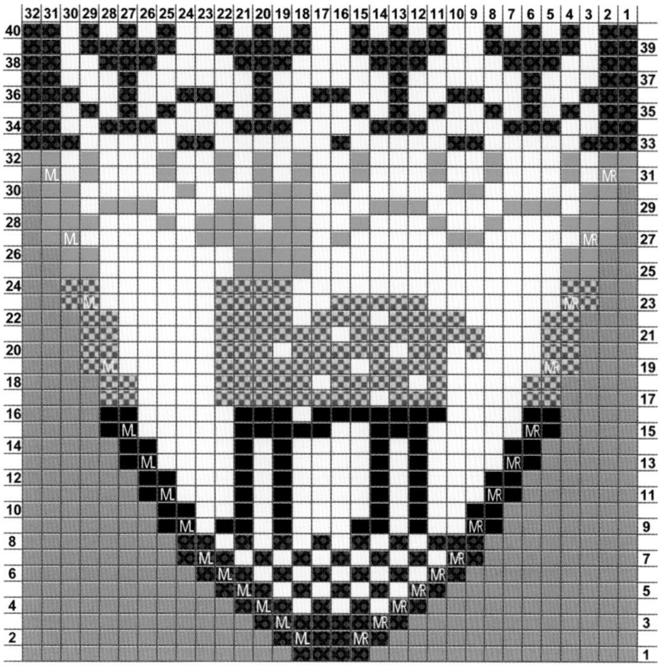

Earflaps—Alpaca—Right

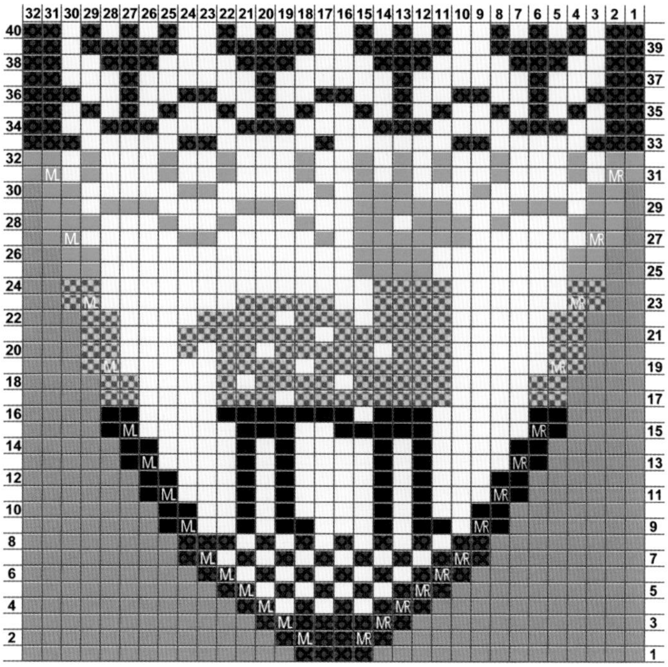

Earflaps—Ripples—Left

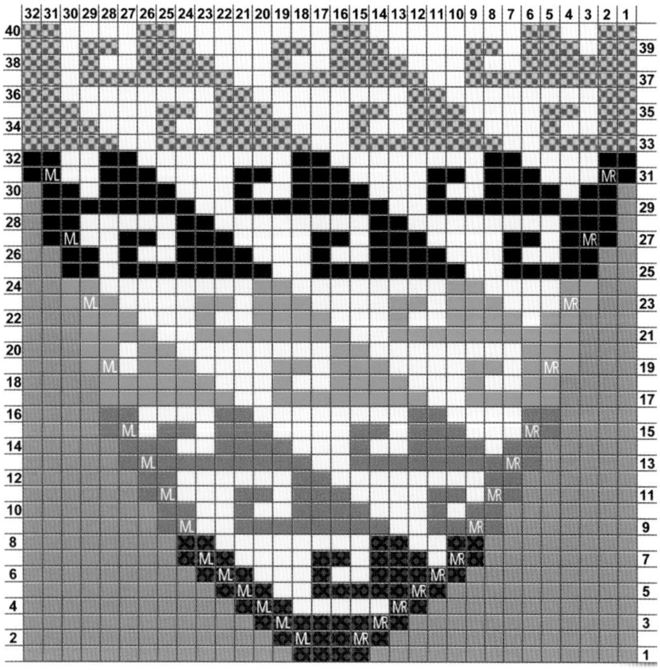

Earflaps—Ripples—Right

Crown—Chain

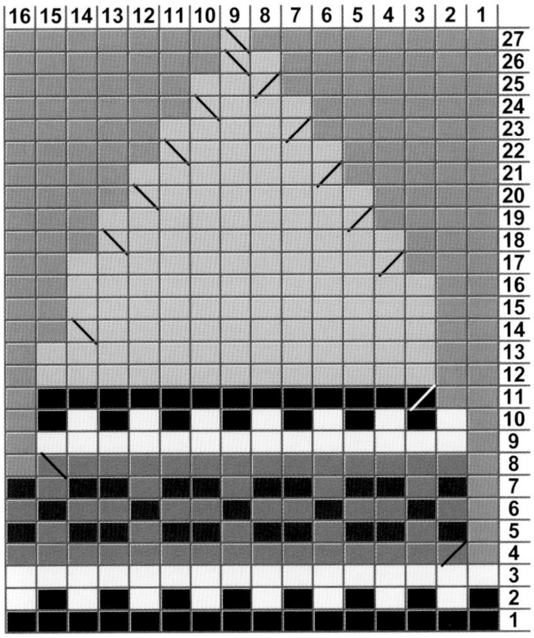

Crown—Coins

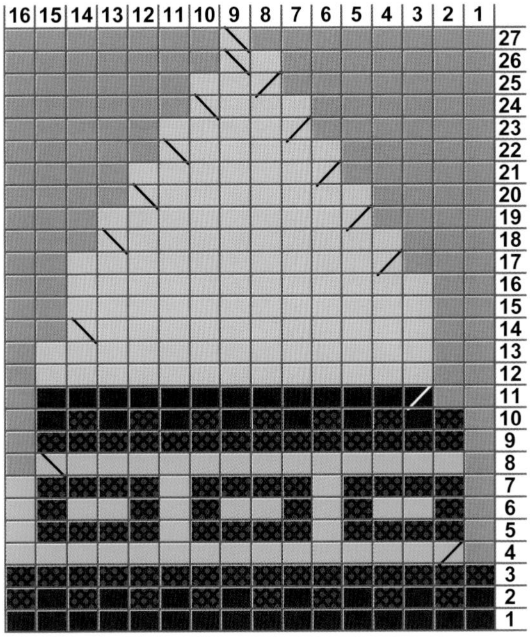

Main Pattern—Alpaca

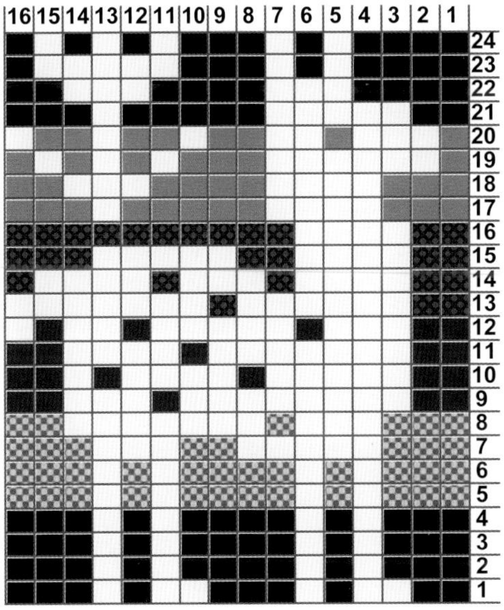

Rep ten times around

Main Pattern—Ripples

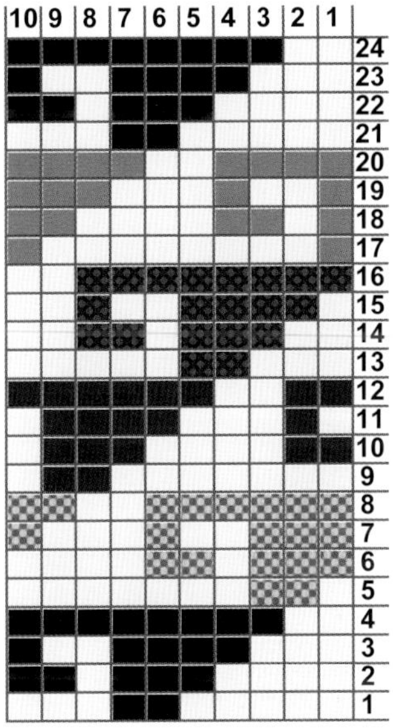

Rep 16 times around

Small Pattern—Dots

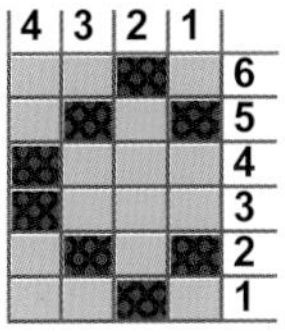

Small Pattern—Flourish

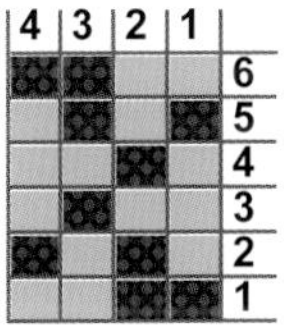

Small Pattern—Little Alpacas

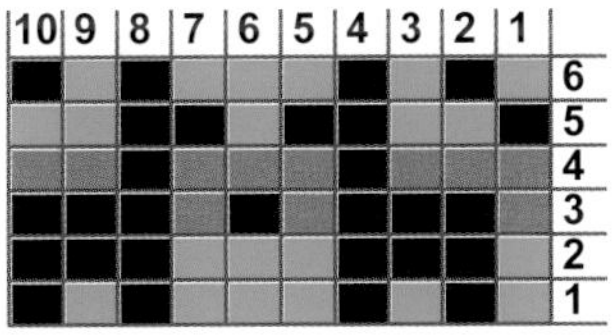

Small Pattern—Spirals

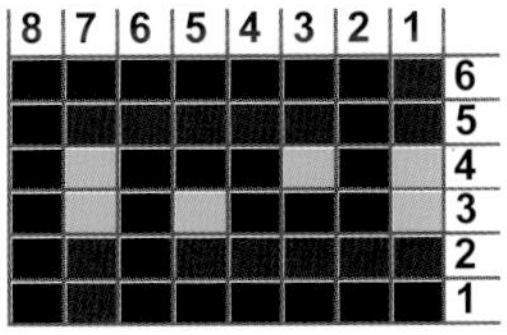

Small Pattern—Tilting Bricks

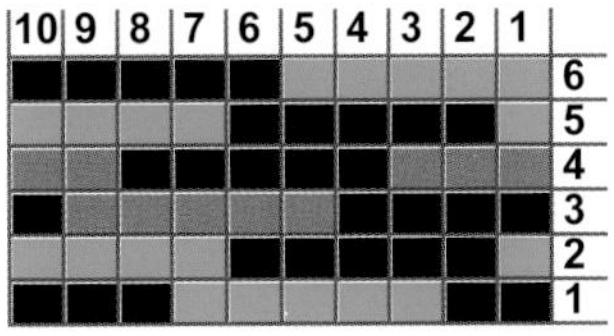

Small Pattern—Little Wave

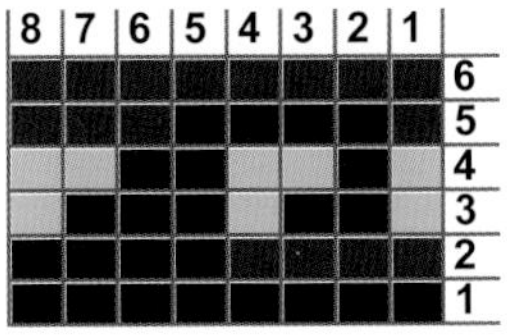

MOUNTAIN SKY COLORWAY

1 ball each:
Silver 24586 (C1)
Delta 24580
Sky 23724
Cyan 24583
Ash 23731
Asphalt Heather 24243
Black 23729
White 23728
Marble Heather 24244

BRIGIT HAT & SCARF

by Nina Isaacson

FINISHED MEASUREMENTS:
Hat: approximately 21″ circumference × 9.5″ height
Scarf: approximately 7.5″ width × 65″ length

YARN
Knit Picks Provincial Tweed™ (worsted weight, 80% Fine Superwash Highland Wool, 20% Donegal Tweed; 250 yards /100g): Candy Apple 27580, 4 hanks
or
Knit Picks Wool of the Andes™ (worsted weight, 100% Peruvian Highland Wool; 220 yards/100g): Bare 23417, 4 hanks

NEEDLES
US 6 (4mm) straight needles, plus DPNs or two 24″ circular needles for two circulars technique or 32″ or longer circular needles for Magic Loop technique, or size to obtain gauge

NOTIONS
Yarn Needle
Stitch Marker
Cable Needle
Pom-Pom (optional)

GAUGE
20 sts and 26 rows = 4″ in Stockinette Stitch, blocked

For pattern support, contact customerservice@knitpicks.com

Brigit Hat & Scarf

Notes:

Cables are easier than they look! The Brigit Hat & Scarf are designed to get you comfortable with cables. Each piece begins with an easy cable pattern and includes an option for a more challenging panel, if you feel up to it! The cloche style hat and elegant scarf are perfect projects for practicing your newfound cable skills.

The charts are worked flat; read RS rows (odd numbers) from right to left, and WS rows (even numbers) from left to right.

HAT DIRECTIONS

Band

CO 30 sts.
Rows 1-4: K across.
Work 17 reps of Hat Chart A.
Work either one rep of Hat Chart B or four more reps of Hat Chart A.
Work three reps of Hat Chart A.
Work Rows 1-3 of Hat Chart A.
Knit across for four rows.
BO all sts.

Join Ends of Band

With RS out, lay BO edge over CO edge, allowing 10 rows to overlap, and sew into place.

Crown

Hold Band horizontally, with BO edge to the left of Chart B panel, and evenly PU and K 104 sts from top selvedge edge. PM for BOR and join to work in the rnd.
Rnds 1-6: K all.

Decreases

Rnd 1: (K11, K2tog) to end. 96 sts.
Rnd 2 and all even numbered rnds: K all.
Rnd 3: (K10, K2tog) to end. 88 sts.
Rnd 5: (K9, K2tog) to end. 80 sts.
Rnd 7: (K8, K2tog) to end. 72 sts.
Rnd 9: (K7, K2tog) to end. 64 sts.
Rnd 11: (K6, K2tog) to end. 56 sts.
Rnd 13: (K5, K2tog) to end. 48 sts.
Rnd 15: (K4, K2tog) to end. 40 sts.
Rnd 17: (K3, K2tog) to end. 32 sts.
Rnd 19: (K2, K2tog) to end. 24 sts.
Rnd 21: (K1, K2tog) to end. 16 sts.
Rnd 23: (K2tog) to end. 8 sts.
Break yarn, thread through remaining sts, pull tight, and fasten off.

Finishing

Weave in ends. Wash and block gently, without creasing. Attach optional pom-pom.

SCARF DIRECTIONS

CO 52 sts.
Rows 1-4: K across.
Work five reps of Scarf Chart A.
Work either one rep of Scarf Chart B or four more reps of Scarf Chart A.
Work 32 reps of Scarf Chart A.
Work either one rep of Scarf Chart B or four more reps of Scarf Chart A (matching how other end of Scarf was worked).
Work five reps of Scarf Chart A.
Work Rows 1-7 of Scarf Chart A.
Knit across for four rows.
BO all sts loosely.

Finishing

Weave in any remaining ends. Wash and block gently, so selvedge edges lie in straight parallel lines.

LEGEND

K
RS: Knit stitch
WS: Purl stitch

P
RS: Purl stitch
WS: Knit stitch

K TBL
RS: Knit stitch through the back loop
WS: Purl stitch through the back loop

Cable 2 Over 1 Right, Purl back (2/1 RPC)
Sl1 to CN, hold in back; K2, P1 from CN

Cable 2 Over 1 Left, Purl back (2/1 LPC)
Sl2 to CN, hold in front; P1, K2 from CN

Cable 2 Over 2 Right (2/2 RC)
Sl2 to CN, hold in back; K2, K2 from CN

Cable 2 Over 2 Left (2/2 LC)
Sl2 to CN, hold in front; K2, K2 from CN

Right Twist (RT)
Sl1 to CN, hold in back; K1, K1 from CN

Left Twist (LT)
Sl1 to CN, hold in front; K1, K1 from CN

Hat Chart A

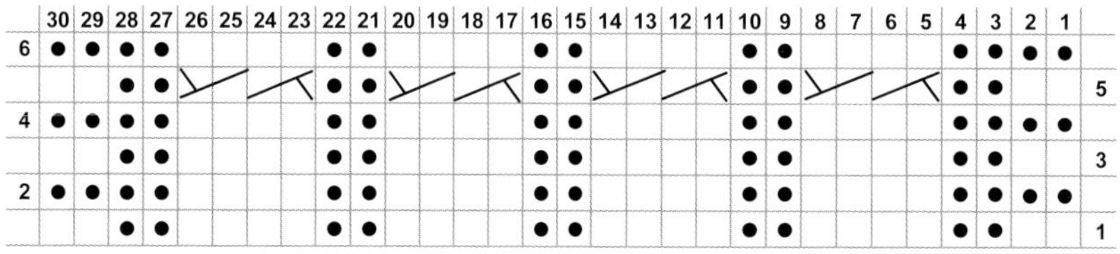

Hat Chart B

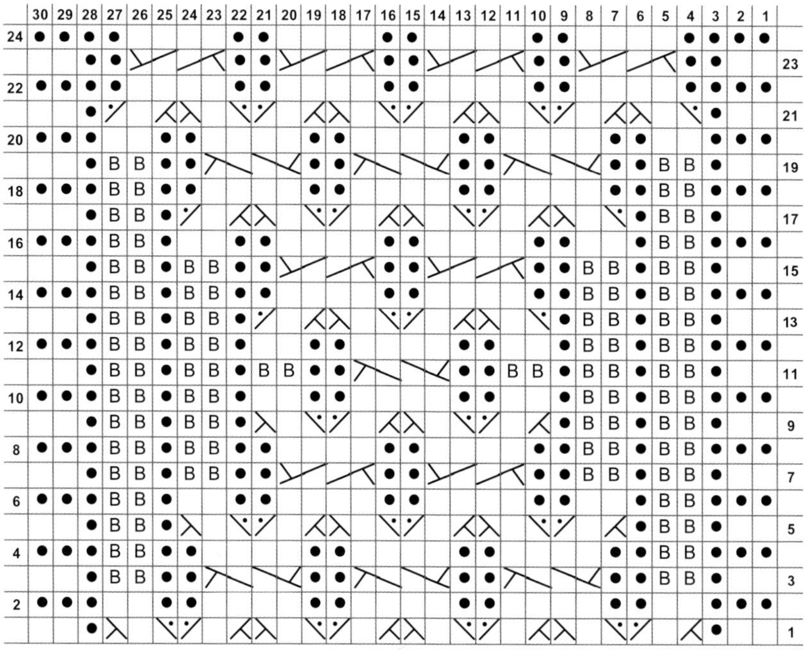

Scarf Chart A

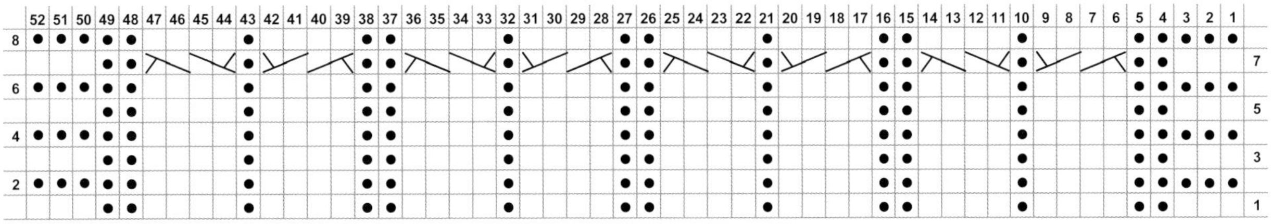

Scarf Chart B

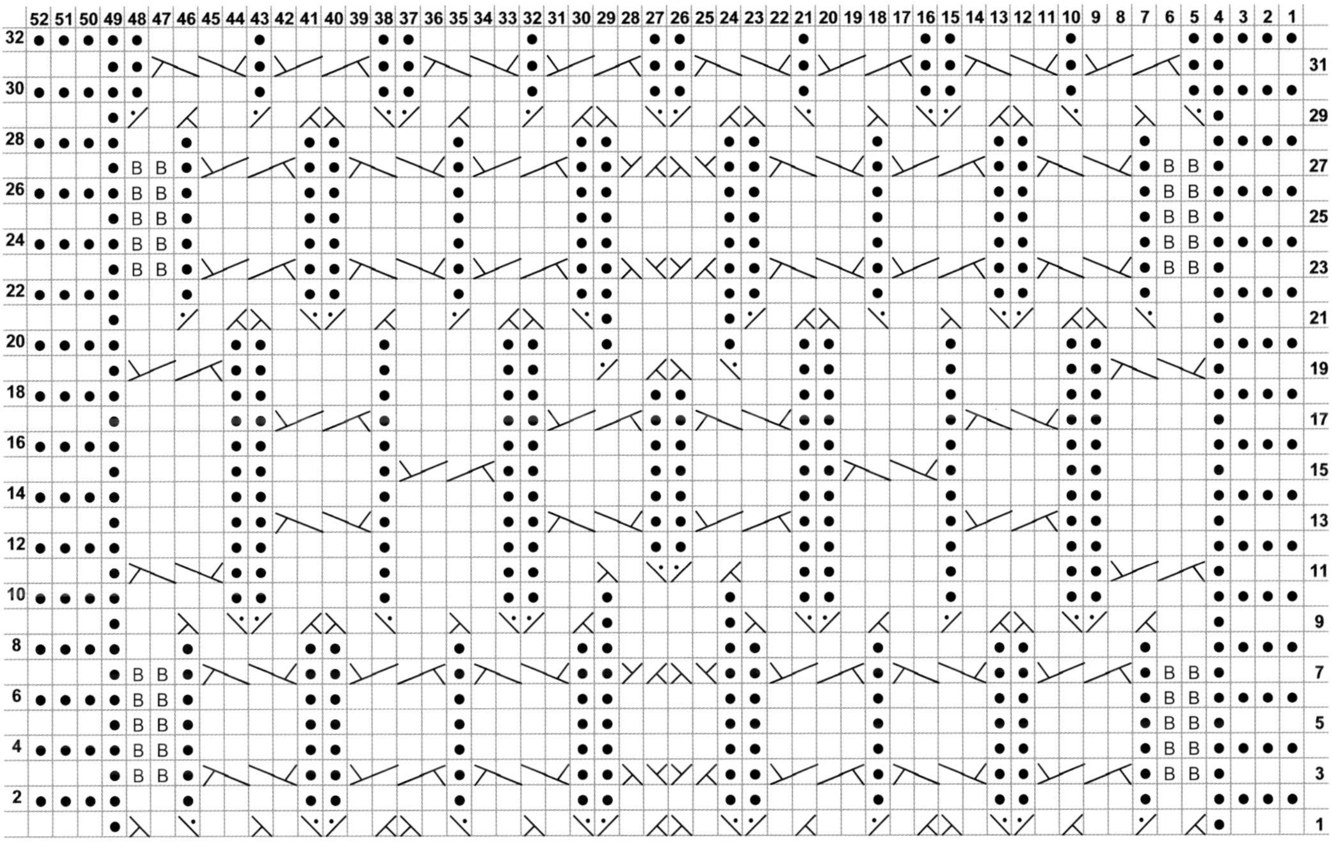

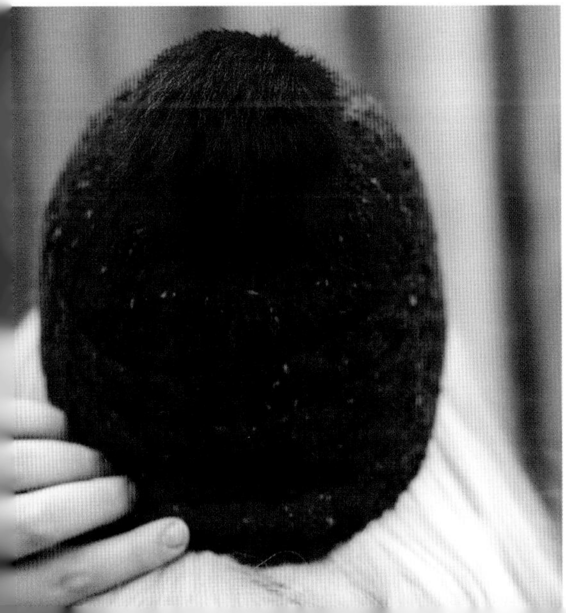

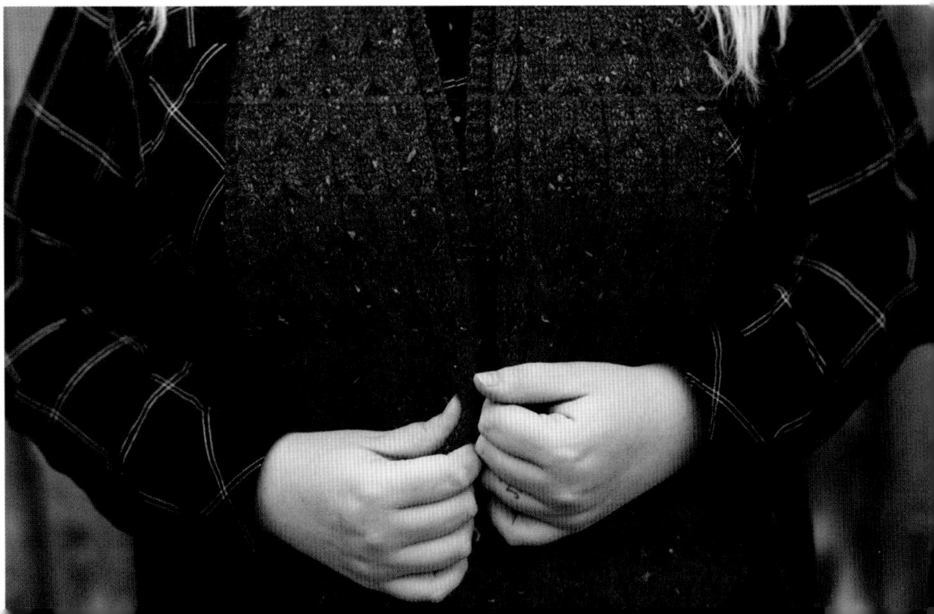

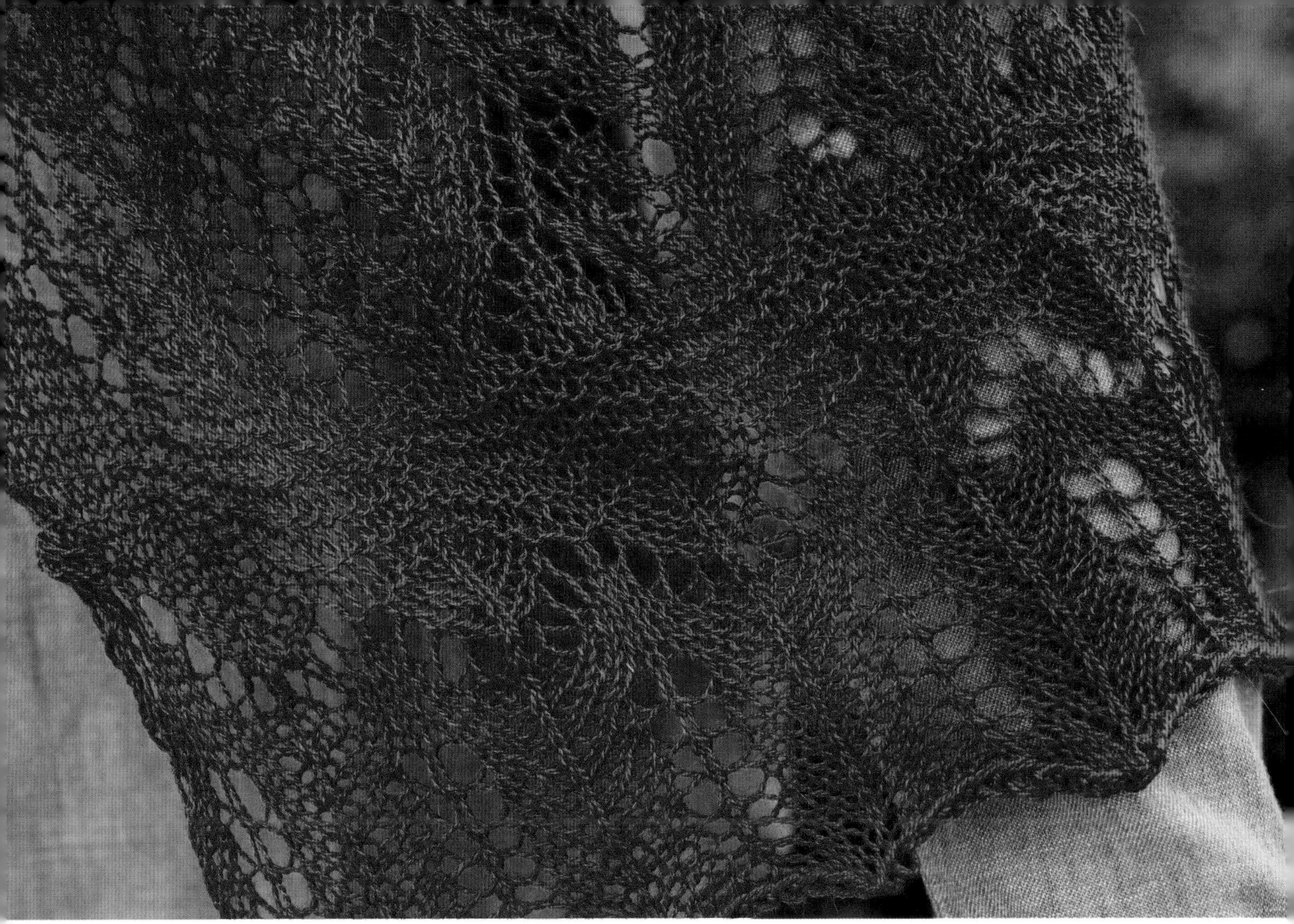

CATKIN SCARF & STOLE

by Kerin Dimeler-Laurence

FINISHED MEASUREMENTS
Scarf: 8.5" × 60"
Stole: 20" × 60"

YARN
Knit Picks Shimmer™ (lace weight, 70% Baby Alpaca, 30% Silk; 440 yards/50g): Rhododendron 27913, 2 hanks
or
Knit Picks Alpaca Cloud™ (lace weight, 100% Baby Alpaca; 440 yards/50g) Elizabeth 26757, 2 hanks
or
Knit Picks Shadow™ (lace weight, 100% Merino Wool; 440 yards/50g) Oregon Coast Heather 23656, 2 hanks

NEEDLES
US 6 (4mm) straight or circular needles, or size to obtain gauge

NOTIONS
Yarn Needle
Stitch Markers

GAUGE
20 sts = 4" in lace patterns, blocked (gauge is approximate and not crucial; block piece to finished measurements)

For pattern support, contact customerservice@knitpicks.com

Catkin Scarf & Stole

Notes:

Make either a scarf or a stole while learning historical Estonian lace stitch patterns in this beautiful design. Keep it traditional by using a subtle neutral yarn, or make yours a modern statement accessory by choosing a bright color!

Catkin Scarf & Stole are knit in one piece, bottom edging to top edging. The patterns are written together with stitch count numbers given as Scarf (Stole).

When working a chart flat, read RS rows (odd numbers) from right to left, and WS rows (even numbers) from left to right.

Casting On

Cast on using a double strand of yarn to create a more sturdy edge that holds its shape. Holding two strands of yarn together, work a Cabled Cast On. Break the second strand after finishing the CO row; weave the ends into this row.

Attaching New Balls of Yarn

Where there is a garter border on a piece, join yarn in these borders and weave the ends in the garter portion. To preserve the appearance of the fabric, yarn should be spliced together when joining a new ball in the larger lace panels. To splice the yarn, fray the last inch of both ends of yarn. (It helps if the yarn has been broken by pulling and not cutting as well.) Place one frayed end over the other so that the entire frayed portions overlap. Using saliva (or water, but saliva works best!) wet the ends of the yarn in your hands and rub vigorously between your palms. Twist the join carefully in the same twist direction as the yarn. Knit this joined section carefully into the work.

K2tog Bind Off

Slip first st to RH needle, *K next st, place 2 sts back onto LH needle and K them tog TBL.
This will create a stretchy edge. Perform this BO using a double strand of yarn. Weave the ends into the BO row.

Nupps

A nupp is a type of bobble that is worked over two rows. It uses YO incs instead of KFB. Nupps have a reputation for being fiddly, but they are really quite simple. The trick is to work them loosely.

To work a 5-Stitch Nupp: K1 into the next st, without slipping the original st off the LH needle, YO loosely, K1 into the same st again, YO, K1 into the same st. 5 sts have been made from 1 st. It may be helpful for you to place markers around nupp sts so that you see where they are on the next row.
On the following WS row, when you come to the 5 nupp sts, purl all 5 sts tog. This is where working YOs loosely is beneficial! If you have trouble purling into all 5 sts at once, purl the first 2 sts tog and then Sl the other sts over P-wise.

DIRECTIONS

Bottom Edging

Using a double strand of yarn and a Cabled Cast On, CO 51 (101) sts.
Work Catkin Bottom Edging Rows 1-24.

Work in Garter st for ten rows, increasing 1 st into each of the first 3 (1) row(s). 54 (102) sts.

Main Body

Next Row (RS): K5, PM, work from Catkin Pattern chart to last 5 sts. (This sets up the garter border.)
(Sl1, K4) over the first 5 sts and K the last 5 sts of every row for the duration of this charted section.
If placing Ms between pattern reps, note that in Rows 7, 9, and 11, the Ms will move 1 st to the left to complete each rep.

Cont on, working Catkin Pattern Rows 1-12 30 times total.

Top Edging

Work in Garter st for ten rows, decreasing 1 st into each of the last 3 (1) row(s). 51 (101) sts.

Work Catkin Top Edging Rows 1-24.
BO all sts using a double strand of yarn and a K2tog Bind Off.

Finishing

Weave in ends, wash.
To block, pin out the points of both bottom and top edges, and each slipped garter edge stitch. This is best done with blocking wires and will create a serrated edge on the sides.

LEGEND

K
RS: Knit stitch
WS: Purl stitch

YO
Yarn over

K2tog
Knit 2 stitches together as one stitch

SSK
Slip, slip, knit slipped stitches together

CDD
Slip first and second stitches together as if to K2tog; knit 1 stitch; pass 2 slipped stitches over the knit stitch

5-Stitch Nupp
Working loosely, into next stitch: (Knit 1, YO) twice, Knit 1

K5tog
RS: Knit 5 stitches together as one
WS: Purl 5 stitches together as one
(These were the 5 Nupp stitches)

Catkin Bottom Edging

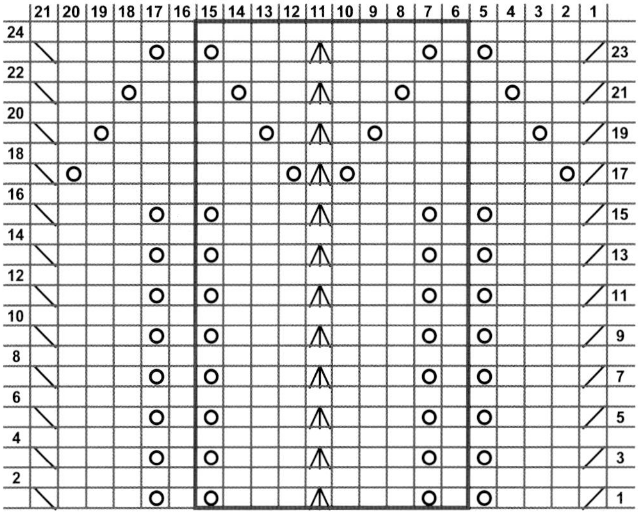

Repeat 4 (9) times

Catkin Pattern

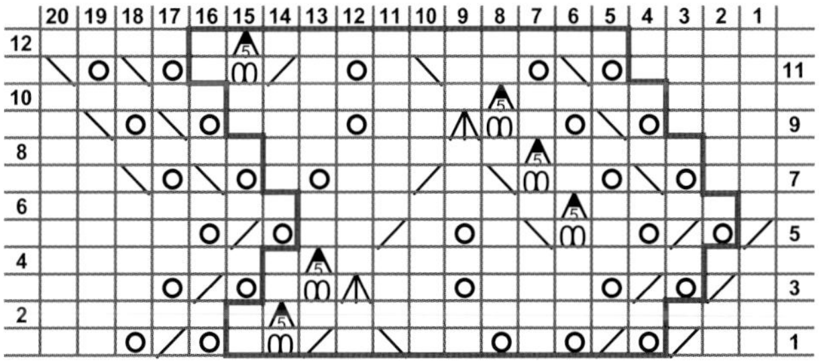

Repeat 3 (7) times

Catkin Top Edging

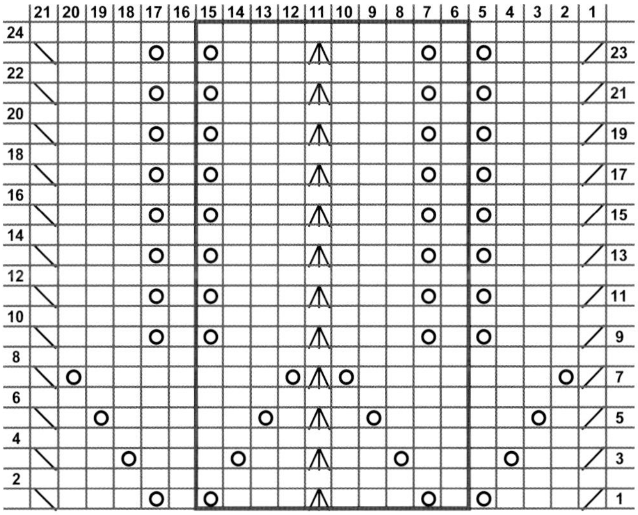

Repeat 4 (9) times

FROST SLIPPERS

by Emily Kintigh

FINISHED MEASUREMENTS
9.5 (10, 10.5)" length

YARN
Knit Picks Wool of the Andes™ (worsted weight, 100% Peruvian Highland Wool; 110 yards/50g): 2 skeins main color, 1 skein each of two contrasting colors (see chart pages for two colorways)

NEEDLES
US 4 (3.5mm) 32" or longer circular needle for Magic Loop technique, or size to obtain gauge

US 3 (3.25mm) DPNs or two 24" circular needles for two circulars technique, or one 32" or longer circular needle for Magic Loop technique, or one size smaller than sized used to obtain gauge

NOTIONS
Yarn Needle
9 Stitch Markers, 1 removable
Size D Crochet Hook

GAUGE
24 sts and 26 rnds = 4" in Stranded Stockinette Stitch in the round on larger needles, blocked

For pattern support, contact customerservice@knitpicks.com

Frost Slippers

Notes:

Keep your toes cozy in a pair of cheerful Frost Slippers! Customize the traditional Nordic design with your favorite color combination.

The slipper tops are worked two at a time using the Magic Loop method with steeks between each slipper and where the cuff will be. The slipper bottoms are also worked two at a time with steeks between them. Once the bottoms and tops are sewn together, stitches are picked up to work the cuff.

The charts are worked in the round; read all rows from right to left as RS rows.

Steeks

To form the steeks, alternate working stitches in each color in the indicated sections on rounds with two colors, in a checkerboard pattern. For single color rows, knit them in the working color.

DIRECTIONS

Slipper Tops

The slipper tops are worked in the round from heel to toe.

With C2, (C1, C2) and larger needles, CO 4 steek sts, PM, CO 11 (12, 13) sts, PM, CO 8 steek sts, PM, CO 11 (12, 13) sts, PM, CO 8 steek sts, PM, CO 11 (12, 13) sts, PM, CO 8 steek sts, PM, CO 11 (12, 13) sts, PM, CO 4 steek sts. 76 (80, 84) sts. Place a removable M here—this M keeps track of BOR and is not counted as one of the Ms indicated below. Join to work in the rnd using Magic Loop method, being careful not to twist sts.

Work the 4 sts before the first M, the sts between second and third Ms, between fourth and fifth Ms, between sixth and seventh Ms, and between eighth M and BOR as steeks. Between first and second Ms, and between fifth and sixth Ms, work Right Chart for your size; between third and fourth Ms, and between seventh and eighth Ms, work Left Chart.

On last rnd of all charts, BO steek sts between second and third Ms, and between sixth and seventh Ms, removing these Ms. 60 (64, 68) sts.

Next Rnd: With C1, K to first section of bound off sts, CO 9 (11, 13) sts, cont knitting to second section of bound off sts, CO 9 (11, 13) sts, K to end. 78 (86, 94) sts.

Toe

Work Toe Chart between first and second Ms, and between third and fourth Ms, while continuing to work steeks before first M, between second and third Ms, and after last M. At end of chart, BO all sts.

Soles

With C2 and larger needles, CO 4 steek sts, PM, CO 4 (6, 8) sts, PM, CO 8 steek sts, PM, CO 4, (6, 8) sts, PM, CO 4 steek sts. 24 (28, 32) sts. Place a removable M—this M keeps track of BOR and is not counted as one of the Ms indicated below. Join to work in the rnd using Magic Loop method, being careful not to twist sts.

Work the 4 sts before first M, the 8 sts between second and third Ms, and the 4 sts after fourth M as steeks, while following row by row directions below for sections between first and second Ms and between third and fourth Ms. Work with C2 except where indicated to work with C1 according to Sole Chart. Steek sts are not included in instructions below, except in st counts.

Rnd 1: K all.
Rnd 2: KFB, K to 1 st before M, KFB. 2 sts inc each non-steek section; 28 (32, 36) sts.
Rnd 3: K2, M1, K to 2 sts before M, M1, K2. 32 (36, 40) sts.
Rnd 4: K all.
Rnd 5: K1, *M1, K3 (4, 5) sts; rep from * once more, M1, K1. 38 (42, 46) sts.
Rnd 6: Join C1 to steek; with C2, K3, work Rnd 1 of Sole Chart to 3 sts before M, K3.
Rnd 7: K1, M1, K1, work Rnd 1 of Sole Chart to 2 sts before M, K1, M1, K1. 42 (46, 50) sts.
Rnd 8: K3, work Rnd 2 of Sole Chart to 3 sts before M, K3.
Rnd 9: K1, M1, K1, work Rnd 2 of Sole Chart to 2 sts before M, K1, M1, K1. 46 (50, 54)
Rnd 10: K3, work Rnd 1 of Sole Chart to 3 sts before M, K3.
Rnd 11: Rep Rnd 7. 50 (54, 58) sts.
Rnd 12: K3, work Rnd 2 of Sole Chart to 3 sts before M, K3.
Rnd 13: K3, work Rnd 1 of Sole Chart to 3 sts before M, K3.

9.5" Size Only

Rnds 14-20: Rep Rnds 12-13 three more times, then Rnd 12 once more.
Rnd 21: Rep Rnd 9. 54 sts.
Rnds 22-30: Rep Rnd 13, then Rnds 12-13 four more times.
Rnd 31: Rep Rnd 7. 58 sts.
Rnds 32-40: Rep Rnds 12-13 four more times, then Rnd 12 once more.
Rnd 41: Rep Rnd 9. 62 sts.
Rnds 42-50: Rep Rnd 13, then Rnds 12-13 four more times.
Move on to Toe Shaping.

10" Size Only

Rnds 14-21: Rep Rnds 12-13.
Rnd 22: Rep Rnd 7. 58 sts.
Rnds 23-32: Rep Rnds 12-13.
Rnd 33: Rep Rnd 7. 62 sts.
Rnds 34-43: Rep Rnds 12-13.
Rnd 44: Rep Rnd 7. 66 sts.
Rnds 45-54: Rep Rnds 12-13.
Move on to Toe Shaping.

10.5" Size Only
Rnds 14-22: Rep Rnds 12-13 four more times, then Rnd 12 once more.
Rnd 23: Rep Rnd 9. 62 sts.
Rnds 24-34: Rep Rnd 13, then Rnds 12-13 five more times.
Rnd 35: Rep Rnd 7. 66 sts.
Rnds 36-46: Rep Rnds 12-13 five more times, then Rnd 12 once more.
Rnd 47: Rep Rnd 9. 70 sts.
Rnds 48-58: Rep Rnd 13, then Rnds 12-13 five more times.
Move on to Toe Shaping.

Toe Shaping

Rnd 1: SSK, K1, work Rnd 2 of Sole Chart to 3 sts before M, K1, K2tog. 58 (62, 66) sts.
Rnd 2: K3, work Rnd 2 of Sole Chart to 3 sts before M, K3.
Rnd 3: SSK, K1, work Rnd 1 of Sole Chart to 3 sts before M, K1, K2tog. 54 (58, 62) sts.
Rnd 4: K3, work Rnd 1 of Sole Chart to 3 sts before M, K3.
Rnds 5-6: Rep Rnd 1. 46 (50, 54) sts.
Rnd 7: Cut C1 and work with C2 only. SSK, K to 2 sts before M, K2tog. 42 (46, 50) sts.
Rnds 8-10: Rep Rnd 7. 30 (34, 38) sts.
BO all sts.

Using crochet hook, reinforce steeks down middles of each steek section. There should be reinforced steeks along both sides of each slipper top, each foot opening, as well as each slipper bottom.
Cut the steeks. Fold over and baste all steeks.

Block all pieces. Using Mattress Stitch seaming along sides, and making invisible horizontal seams at toe and back of heel, sew Sole to Slipper Top with WSs tog and starting at toe and working back towards heel.
Sew the two sides of CO edge of Slipper Top tog to form back of heel.
Rep for second slipper.

Cuffs

With MC and smaller needles, PU and K 56 (60, 64) sts around opening for foot, PM for BOR.
Work 2x2 Rib until cuff measures 6" long, or desired length. For a cuff that does not fold over, work until cuff measures 3" long.
Loosely BO all sts.
Rep for second slipper.

Finishing

Weave in any remaining ends, and block again if desired.

LEGEND: BLUE COLORWAY

No Stitch
Placeholder—no stitch made

Main Color (White)

Contrasting Color 1 (Fjord Heather)

Contrasting Color 2 (Icicle Heather)

Knit Stitch

M1
Make 1 stitch

K2tog
Knit 2 stitches together as one stitch

SSK
Slip, slip, knit slipped stitches together

9.5″ size
Work outlined section, working decs with yarn indicated

10″ size
Work outlined section, working decs with yarn indicated

10.5″ size
Work outlined section, working decs with yarn indicated

Pattern Repeat

9.5″ Right Chart

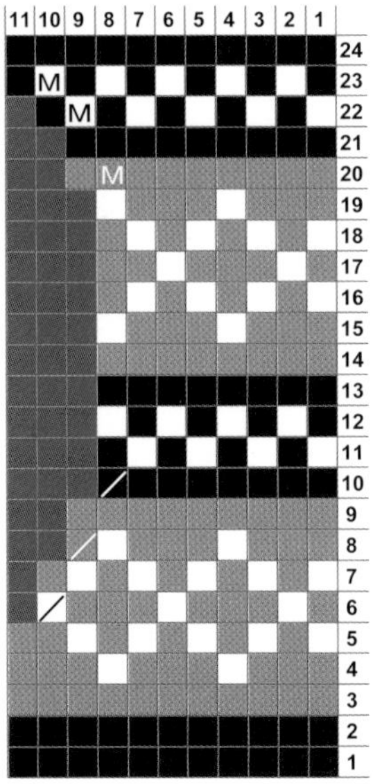

9.5″ Left Chart

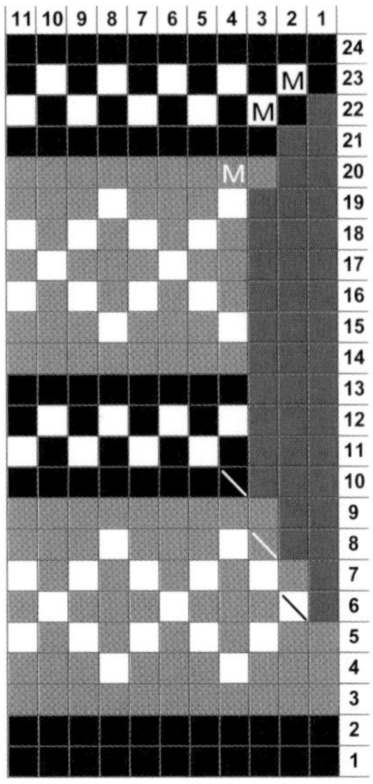

10″ Right Chart

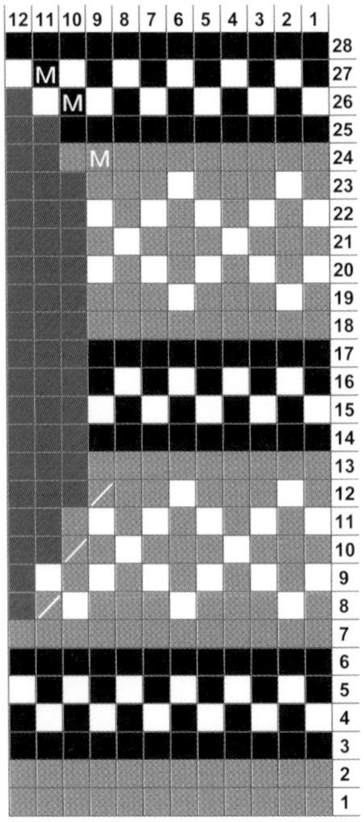

10″ Left Chart

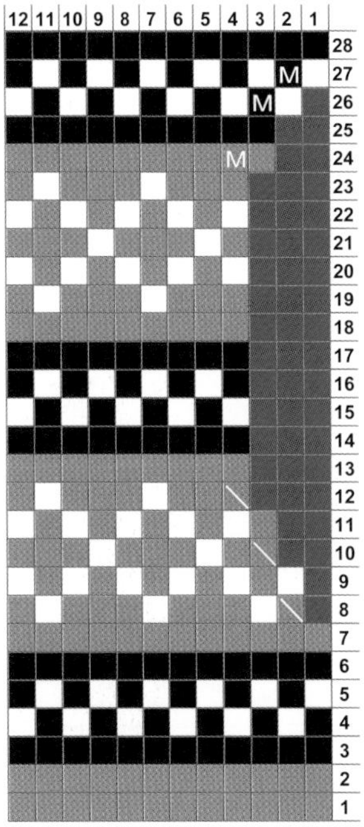

10.5″ Right Chart

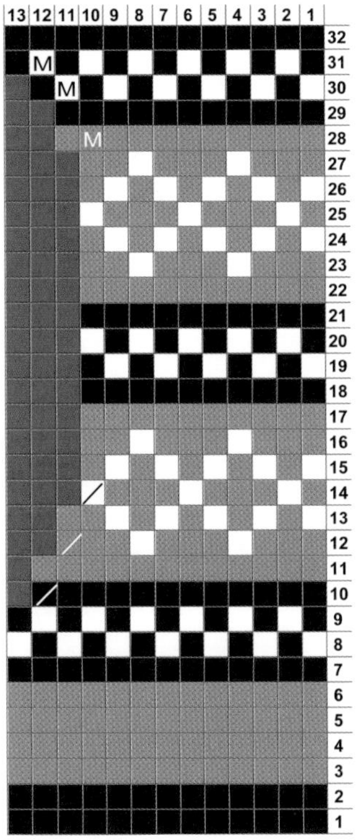

10.5″ Left Chart

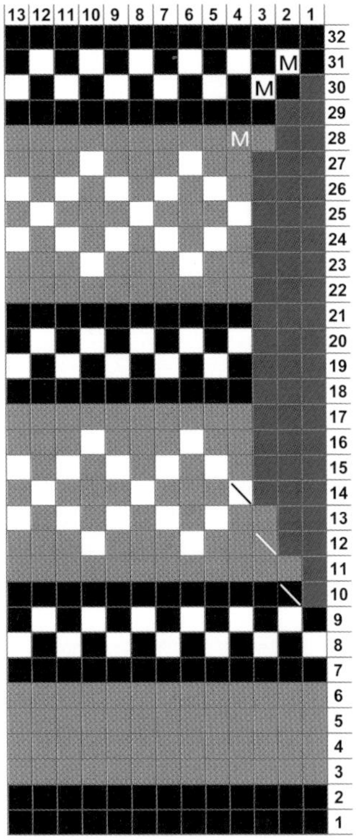

Toe Chart

Sole Chart

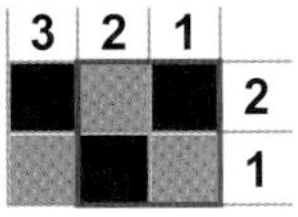

BLUE COLORWAY

2 skeins:
MC White 24065

1 skein each:
C1 Fjord Heather 25647
C2 Icicle Heather 25992

LEGEND: RED COLORWAY

No Stitch
Placeholder—no stitch made

Main Color (White)

Contrasting Color 1 (Hollyberry)

Contrasting Color 2 (Grizzly Heather)

Knit Stitch

M1
Make 1 stitch

K2tog
Knit 2 stitches together as one stitch

SSK
Slip, slip, knit slipped stitches together

9.5″ size
Work outlined section, working decs with yarn indicated

10″ size
Work outlined section, working decs with yarn indicated

10.5″ size
Work outlined section, working decs with yarn indicated

Pattern Repeat

9.5″ Right Chart

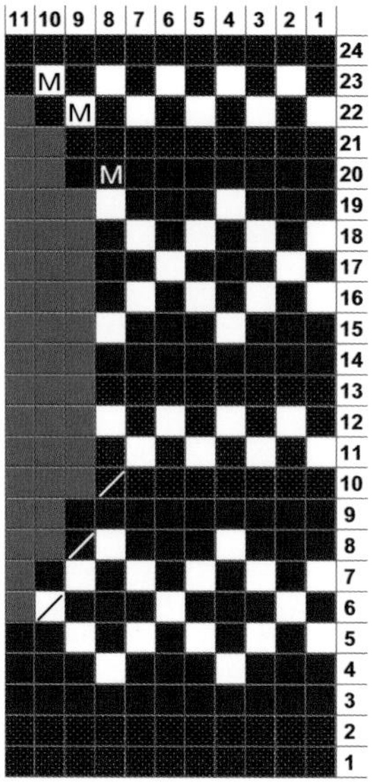

9.5″ Left Chart

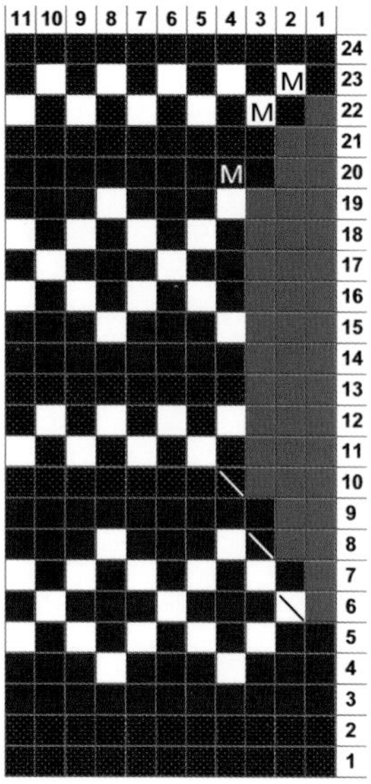

10″ Right Chart

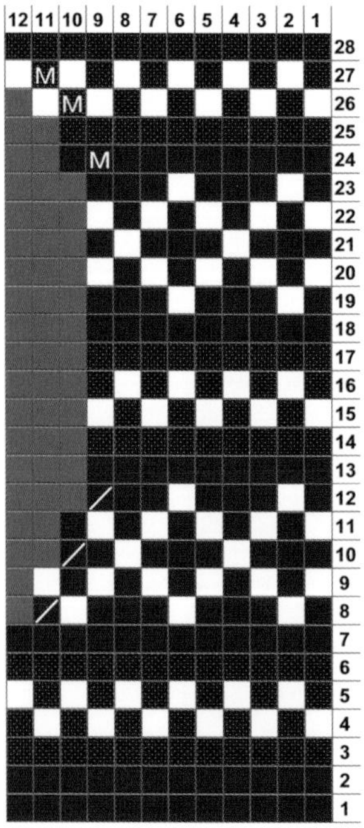

10″ Left Chart

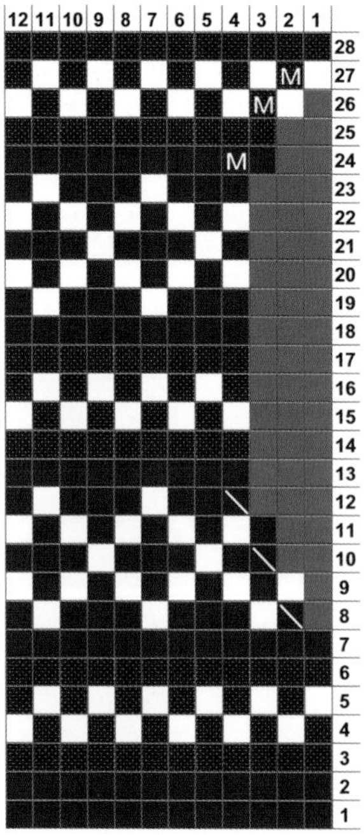

10.5″ Right Chart

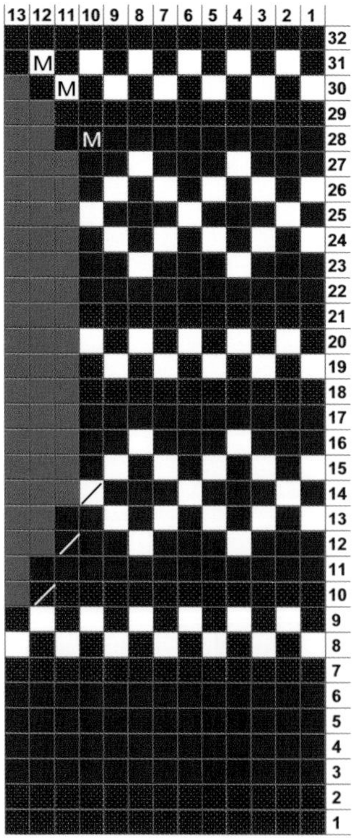

10.5″ Left Chart

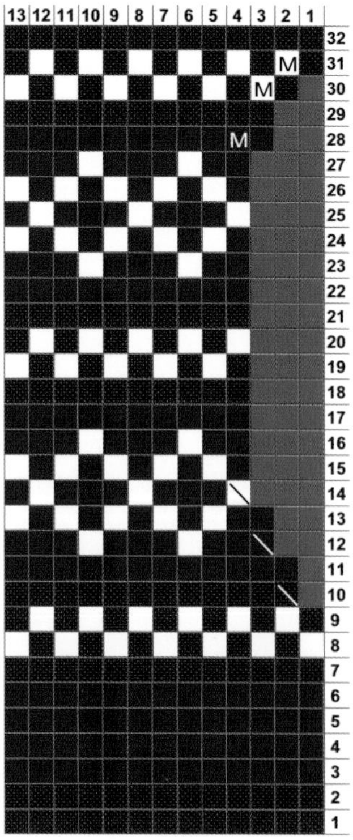

Toe Chart

Sole Chart

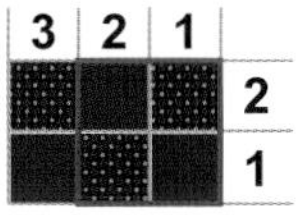

RED COLORWAY

2 skeins:
MC White 24065

1 skein each:
C1 Hollyberry 23419
C2 Grizzly Heather 25641

GRADUAL RIB HAT

by Kerin Dimeler-Laurence

FINISHED MEASUREMENTS

19" (unstretched) circumference × 8.25" height

YARN

Knit Picks Hawthorne™ Tonal & Multi (fingering weight, 75% Fine Superwash Highland Wool, 25% Nylon; 357 yards/100g)

Warm: MC Hood River Tonal 27405, CC Kenton Multi 27414, 1 hank each

Blue & Pink: MC Irvington Multi 26439, CC Rose City Multi 26432, 1 hank each

or

Knit Picks Stroll™ (fingering weight, 75% Fine Superwash Merino Wool, 25% Nylon; 231 yards/50g)

Neutrals: MC Navy 23694, CC Jack Rabbit Heather 25610, 1 skein each

NEEDLES

US 1 (2.25mm) straight or circular needles, or size to obtain gauge

NOTIONS

Yarn Needle

GAUGE

30 sts and 32 rows = 4" in Garter Stitch, blocked

For pattern support, contact customerservice@knitpicks.com

Gradual Rib Hat

Notes:

Intarsia meets Garter Stitch in this visually interesting hat. It is worked sideways by knitting all rows and utilizing short rows to shape the crown. After the last section is knit, a seam closes the hat.

Two rows of Garter Stitch equals one Garter Ridge. Each row in the chart represents one Ridge, comprised of one RS row and one WS row which is the same chart row worked left to right. When working WS rows (brim to crown), you'll wrap and turn on the last MC stitch of the Ridge, ending that Ridge; work RS rows back to brim, beginning the next Ridge.

After Ridge 13, as you work each WS row, pick up the wraps and work them together with the stitches they wrap.

DIRECTIONS

Sts are CO in both colors. Consider the CO row to be the WS row of Ridge 26—it is the pair to the RS Row 51 that will make up the seam. Row 1 after CO is the RS row of the first Garter Ridge on the chart.

Using a Cabled Cast On, CO 11 sts in CC and 51 sts in MC. 62 sts.

Work from Gradual Rib Chart starting on Row 1, the RS of Ridge 1, working short rows as directed, and changing colors where noted. Wrap yarns around each other at color boundaries on each row.

Work through end of chart, then work five more full chart reps, ending with the RS of Ridge 26 (Row 51).
Break both colors, leaving long tails for seaming.

Seam Hat

Turn hat inside out. With a yarn needle, seam or graft the two edges of the hat closed, grafting live sts to CO edge in Garter Stitch, following color pattern on Ridge 26 of chart.

Finishing

Weave in ends, wash, and block to finished measurements.

Gradual Rib Chart

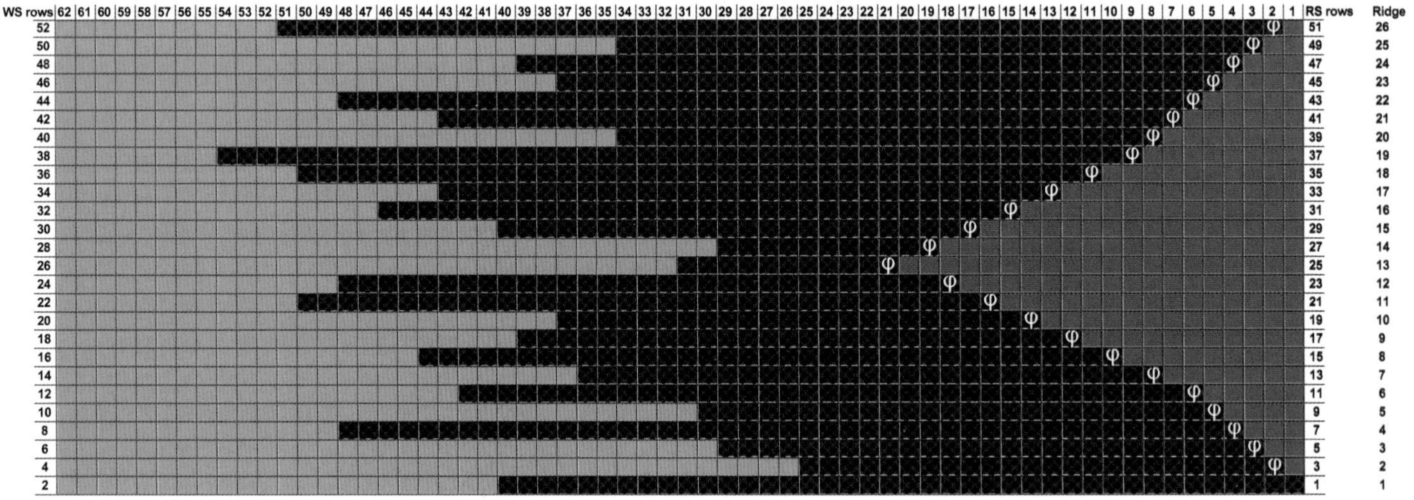

LEGEND

- No Stitch
  Placeholder—no stitch made
- **Main Color (Hood River *or* Irvington *or* Navy)**
- **Contrasting Color (Kenton *or* Rose City *or* Jack Rabbit Heather)**
- **Knit Stitch**
- **W&T**
  Wrap and turn for short row

LAMPWORK HAT & MITTS

by Kerin Dimeler-Laurence

FINISHED MEASUREMENTS
Hat: 18.75 (21.25)" brim circumference × 11.5" height
Mitts: 6.25, (7.5, 8.5)" palm circumference × 10.5 (11.25, 12)" length, to fit Women's S, M, L; see sizing notes in pattern

YARN
Hat: Knit Picks Wool of the Andes™ (worsted weight, 100% Peruvian Highland Wool; 110 yards/50g): 1 skein each of three colors (see chart pages for three colorways)
Mitts: Knit Picks Wool of the Andes™ (sport weight, 100% Peruvian Highland Wool; 137 yards/50g): 1 skein each of three colors (see chart pages for three colorways)

NEEDLES
Hat: US 8 (5mm) DPNs or 32-60" circular needles for Magic Loop, or size to obtain gauge
US 7 (4.5mm) DPNs or 32-60" circular needles for Magic Loop, or one size smaller than size used to obtain gauge
Mitts: US 5 (3.75mm) DPNs or 32-60" circular needles for Magic Loop, or size to obtain gauge
US 4 (3.5mm) DPNs or 32-60" circular needles for Magic Loop, or one size smaller than size used to obtain gauge

NOTIONS
Yarn Needle
Stitch Markers
Smooth Scrap Yarn
Extra DPNs or Circular Needle

GAUGE
Hat: 18 sts and 20 rnds = 4" in Stranded Stockinette Stitch in the round, blocked
Mitts: 28 sts and 30 rnds = 4" in Stranded Stockinette Stitch in the round, blocked

For pattern support, contact customerservice@knitpicks.com

Lampwork Hat & Mitts

Notes:

The Lampwork Hat & Mitts are a colorful, coordinating accessory set that feature the same bright patterning, worked in the same colors at different gauges. The hat uses Wool of the Andes Worsted and is worked as a simple beanie with ribbing at the brim, while a deep chevron pattern transitions into what seem like panels of stained glass along the crown. The mitts use the lighter weight Wool of the Andes Sport; right and left are worked identically to each other except for thumb placement. Like the hat's brim, the mitts start with a wide ribbed cuff.

Both the hat and mitts feature a colorful allover patterning where three strands of yarn are worked across a single row at times. Because the triple-stranded colorwork tends to make a less-stretchy fabric, the mitts are large through the palm and the pattern also includes tips on sizing.

To choose your mitt size, measure around your hand, including the thumb, at the base of the thumb. If this measurement is closest to 7", work size Small; if closest to 8", work size Medium; if closest to 9", work size Large directions. This affects how many stitches to cast on and pattern repeats to work.

HAT DIRECTIONS

With worsted weight MC and smaller needles, loosely CO 84 (96) sts. PM and join to work in the rnd, being careful not to twist sts.
Work 2x2 Rib for 2-4", depending on your preference.
Next Rnd: Switch to larger needles, K all.

Attach worsted weight C1 and work Allover Chart, repeating chart sts 21 (24) times around. Work 9-rnd chart three times.

Work Crown Chart, repeating chart sts 7 (8) times around, and following decs as given in chart.
After last rnd, 7 (8) sts remain. Break CCs.
Next Rnd: K2tog to last 1 (0) st, K 1 (0). 4 sts.
Break MC and pass yarn tail through remaining live sts; pull tight to close hole.

Finishing

Weave in ends, wash, and block.

MITTS DIRECTIONS

With sport weight MC and smaller needles, loosely CO 44 (52, 60) sts. PM and join to work in the rnd, being careful not to twist sts.
Work 2x2 Rib for 2-4", depending on your preference.
Next Rnd: Switch to larger needles, K all.

Attach sport weight C1 and work Mitt Chart, repeating chart sts 11 (13, 15) times around. Colorwork portion begins at base of palm; measure your hand to base of your fingers. If palm measures closest to 4", work size Small; closest to 4.5", work Medium size; closest to 5", work Large size. This affects how many rnds to knit and where to place Thumb.

Thumb & Top of Mitt

In the rnd indicated for your size, an afterthought thumb is set up. For right mitt, first work 2 sts in pattern; for left mitt, work in pattern to 10 sts before end of rnd.
For both mitts: with scrap yarn, K8, Sl these 8 sts back to LH needle; cont working in pattern with working yarns across these 8 sts and around hand.

Cont working in the rnd to last chart rnd for your size.
Break CCs and knit one rnd in MC.
Switch to smaller needles and work 2x2 Rib for 1".
BO all sts loosely.

Place the 8 sts below afterthought thumb onto one smaller-size DPN or one side of a circular needle. On a second DPN or the other side of a circular needle, place the 8 sts from the row above the afterthought thumb. Unravel the scrap yarn, leaving a hole and 16 live sts.
Attach MC, PM, and K around all sts using smaller needles; join to work in the rnd.
Work 2x2 Rib for 1".
BO all sts loosely. Using yarn tails, close up any holes at sides of thumb ribbing.

Second Mitt

Make second mitt same as first, changing thumb position.

Finishing

Weave in ends, wash, and block.

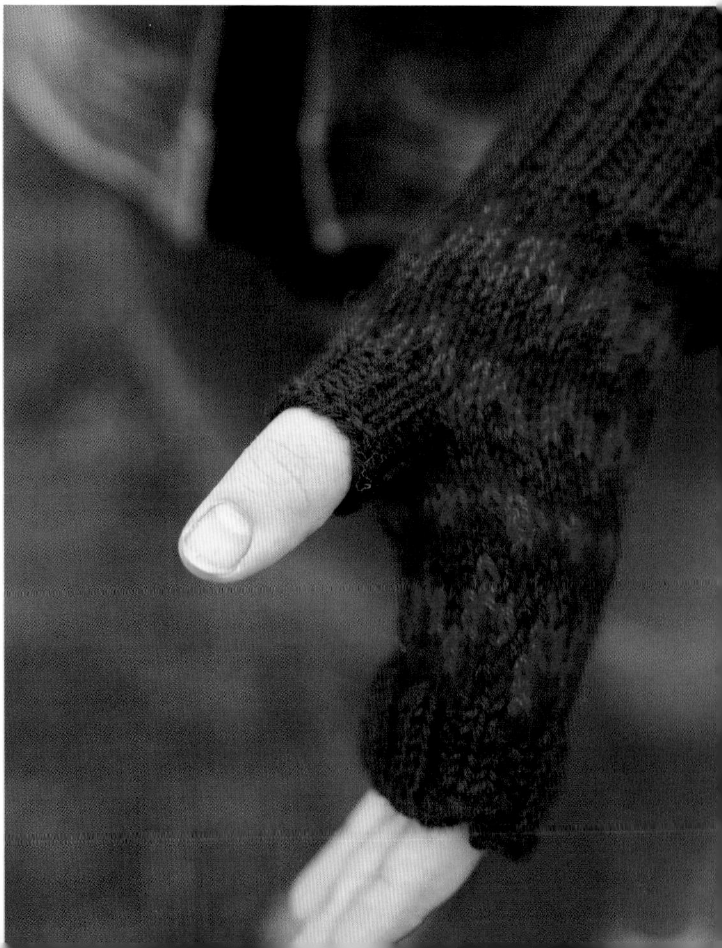

LEGEND: RED COLORWAY

No Stitch
Placeholder—no stitch made

Main Color (Blackberry)

Contrasting Color 1 (Hollyberry)

Contrasting Color 2 (Red)

Knit Stitch

K2tog
Knit 2 stitches together as one stitch

SSK
Slip, slip, knit slipped stitches together

CDD
Slip first and second stitches together as if to K2tog; knit 1 stitch; pass 2 slipped stitches over the knit stitch

RED COLORWAY

For hat, 1 skein each:
MC Blackberry 24273
C1 Hollyberry 23419
C2 Red 23764

For mitts, 1 skein each:
MC Blackberry 25300
C1 Hollyberry 25298
C2 Red 25297

Allover Chart

Crown Chart

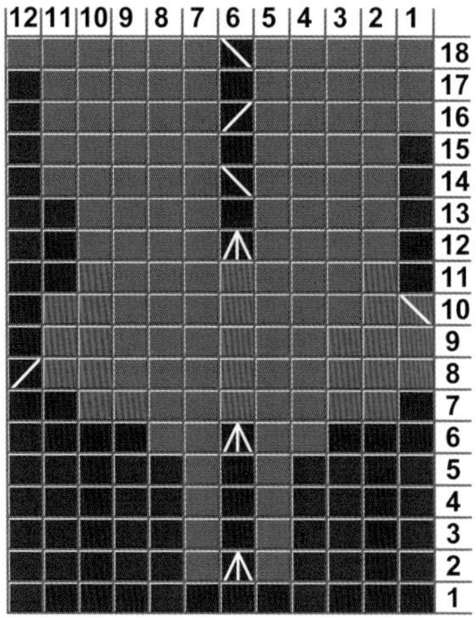

Mitt Chart

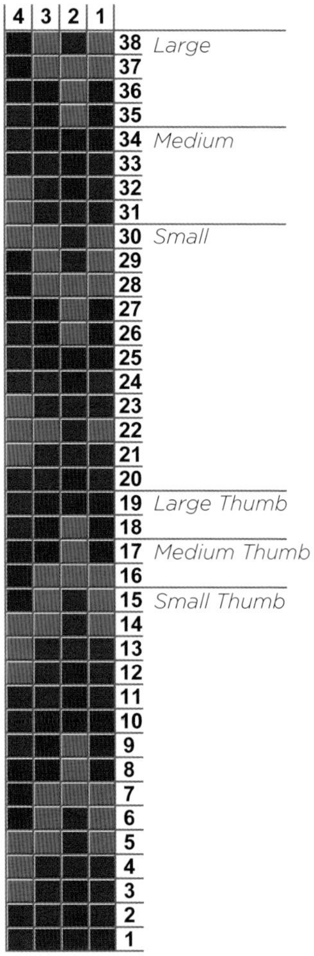

LEGEND: GREEN COLORWAY

No Stitch
Placeholder—no stitch made

Main Color (Aurora Heather)

Contrasting Color 1 (Marina)

Contrasting Color 2 (Avocado)

Knit Stitch

K2tog
Knit 2 stitches together as one stitch

SSK
Slip, slip, knit slipped stitches together

CDD
Slip first and second stitches together as if to K2tog; knit 1 stitch; pass 2 slipped stitches over the knit stitch

GREEN COLORWAY

For hat, 1 skein each:
MC Aurora Heather 25065
CC1 Marina 25074
CC2 Avocado 23766

For mitts, 1 skein each:
MC Aurora Heather 25299
CC1 Marina (can substitute Baltic Heather 25655)
CC2 Avocado (can substitute Green Tea Heather 25281)

Mitt Chart

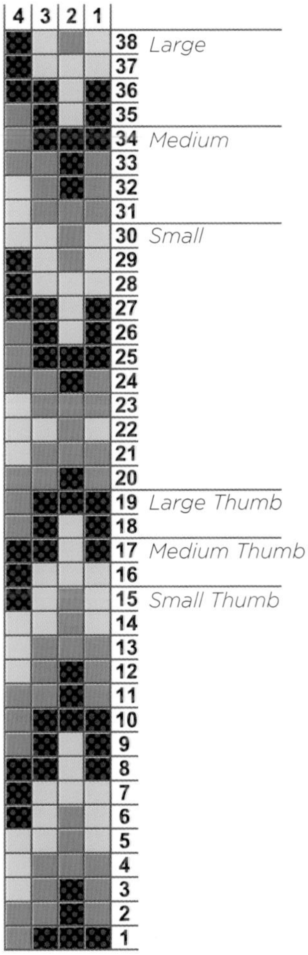

Allover Chart

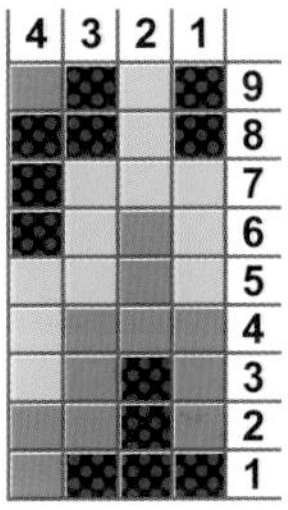

Crown Chart

LEGEND: NEUTRAL COLORWAY

No Stitch
Placeholder—no stitch made

Main Color (Chestnut)

Contrasting Color 1 (Mink Heather)

Contrasting Color 2 (Oyster Heather)

Knit Stitch

K2tog
Knit 2 stitches together as one stitch

SSK
Slip, slip, knit slipped stitches together

CDD
Slip first and second stitches together as if to K2tog; knit 1 stitch; pass 2 slipped stitches over the knit stitch

NEUTRAL COLORWAY

For hat, 1 skein each:
MC Chestnut 23424
C1 Mink Heather 24279
C2 Oyster Heather 24649

For mitts, 1 skein each:
MC Chestnut 25273
C1 Mink Heather 25275
C2 Oyster Heather 25276

Mitt Chart

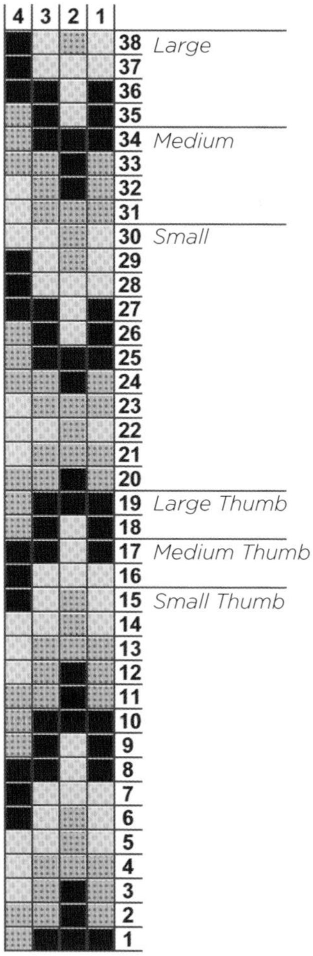

Allover Chart

Crown Chart

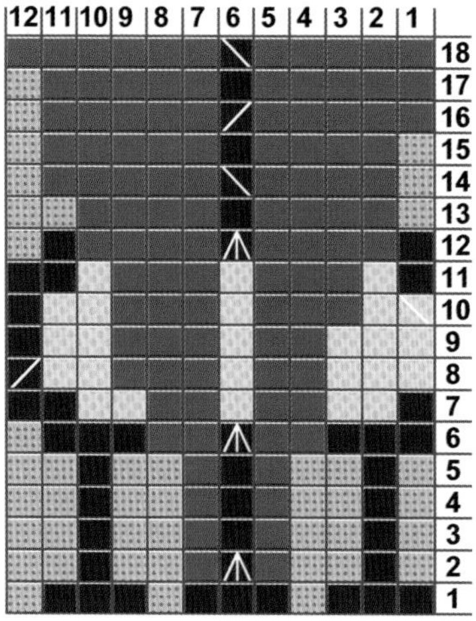

SHIFT TOTE

by Kerin Dimeler-Laurence

FINISHED MEASUREMENTS
15″ height × 4″ depth × 12″ width (not including handles)

YARN
Knit Picks Wool of the Andes™ (worsted weight, 100% Peruvian Highland Wool; 110 yards/50g): MC Onyx Heather 24076, 2 skeins
and Knit Picks Chroma™ (worsted weight, 70% Wool, 30% Nylon; 198 yards/100g): C1 Lupine 26471, C2 Pegasus 26554, 1 ball each
or
Alternative Colorway 1: (same yarn lines & quantities) MC Coal 23420; C1 Red Velvet 26469, C2 Drawing Room 26934
or
Alternative Colorway 2: (same yarn lines & quantities) MC Icicle Heather 25992; C1 Surf's Up 26933, C2 Wednesday 28056

NEEDLES
US 7 (4.5mm) 24″ circular needles or longer for Magic Loop method, or size to obtain gauge
US 6 (4mm) straight or short circular needles, or one size smaller than size used to obtain gauge

NOTIONS
Yarn Needle
Stitch Markers
Crochet Hook and Scrap Yarn for Provisional Cast On
Yarn Bobbins (optional)

GAUGE
18 sts and 26 rows = 4″ in Stockinette Stitch on larger needles, blocked

For pattern support, contact customerservice@knitpicks.com

Shift Tote

Notes:
This fun tote takes advantage of Chroma's gently shifting colors to make a visually enticing article. The bottom and trim are worked in Garter Stitch with Wool of the Andes, while the body is worked in Stockinette Stitch in the intarsia technique with two colorways of Chroma.

Before beginning Intarsia Body, make eight roughly equal balls from each C1 and C2. These will be used throughout the bag, each being cut at one end and reattached at the other as the chevrons pass by the edges of the bag. Try winding some of these balls from either end of the main ball of yarn; this can really mix up the color variations.

The piece is entirely worked flat; the chart is read right to left on RS rows and left to right on WS rows.

DIRECTIONS

Base

Using larger needles, scrap yarn, and Provisional Cast On, CO 51 sts.
Attach MC.
Row 1 (RS): K across.
Row 2 (WS): KFB, K to last st, KFB. 2 sts inc; 53 sts.
Rep Rows 1-2 three more times. 59 sts.
Rows 9-30: K across.
Row 31: K2tog, K to last 2 sts, K2tog. 2 sts dec; 57 sts.
Row 32: K across.
Rep Rows 31-32 three more times. 51 sts.

Upper Base
Setup Row (RS): Turn work and knit across these live sts; without turning work, PU and K 1 st into each Garter ridge around adjacent curved edge (19 sts); undo Provisional CO and place original 51 sts on a spare needle, knit across these sts with working yarn; as for first curved edge, PU and K 19 sts around remaining edge. 140 sts.
Rows 1-9: Work Garter st.

Intarsia Body

Work Shift Chart, beginning with Row 1 (RS); rep the 20-st chart seven times across bag. Attach a new ball of yarn at each color transition. The first row will contain 14 separate balls of yarn.

Work chart back and forth in St st, wrapping yarns around each other at each color transition. As one section of color runs off the edge, break that yarn and reattach it when the next stripe of that color begins on the other side.

Top Border

After last chart row, slide all sts back to other end of needle, ready to work another RS row. Attach MC and knit across all sts, breaking each of the balls of C1 and C2 as you go.
Rows 1-9: Work Garter st.
BO all sts.

Finishing

Seaming
With MC, using Mattress Stitch, seam the two open edges tog, matching chevron pattern and Garter st borders.
Weave in ends.

Handles (make two the same)
With MC and smaller needles, CO 50 sts, leaving a long CO tail. Work Garter st for 1".
BO all sts, leaving a long tail.
Using CO and BO tails for each handle, stitch each end of handle to inside of upper edge of bag, following placement diagram.

Wash and block. If desired for shaping, stuff tote with plastic bags while drying.

Shift Chart

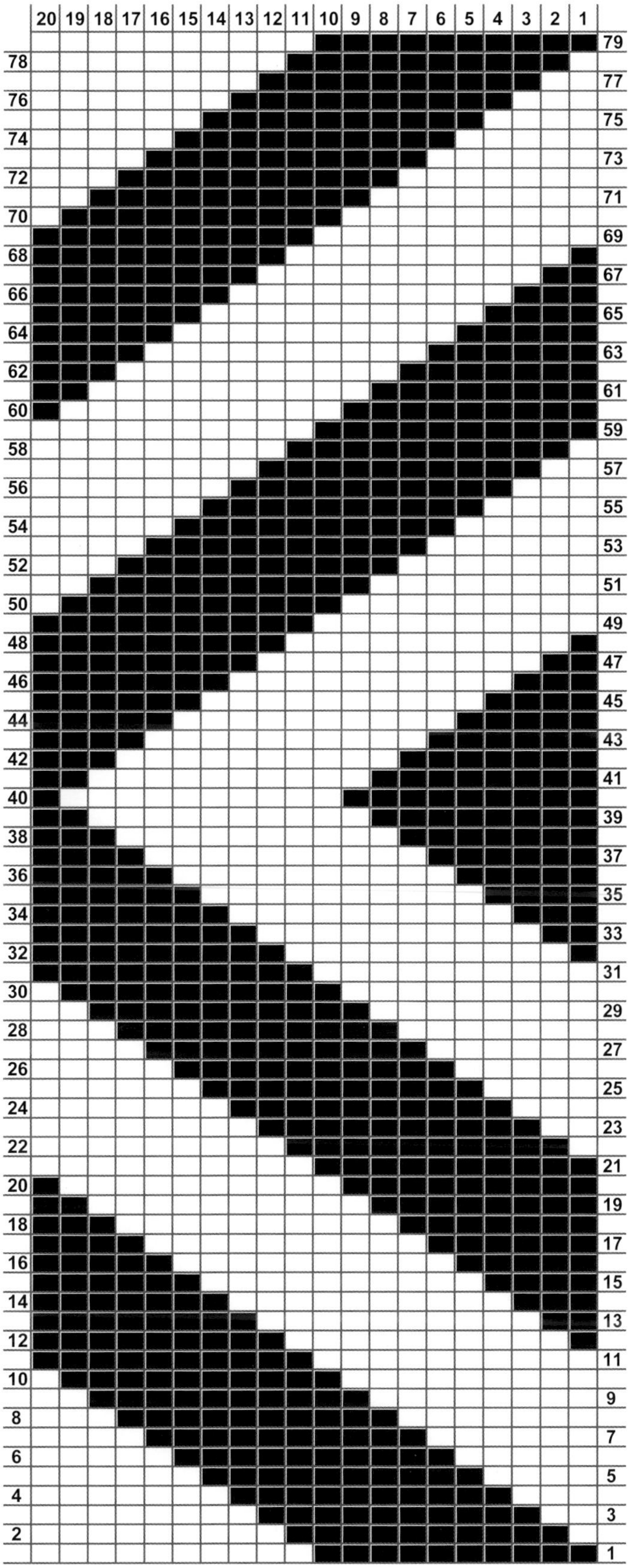

LEGEND

- ■ C1 (Contrasting Color 1)
- □ C2 (Contrasting Color 2)

Handle Placement Diagram

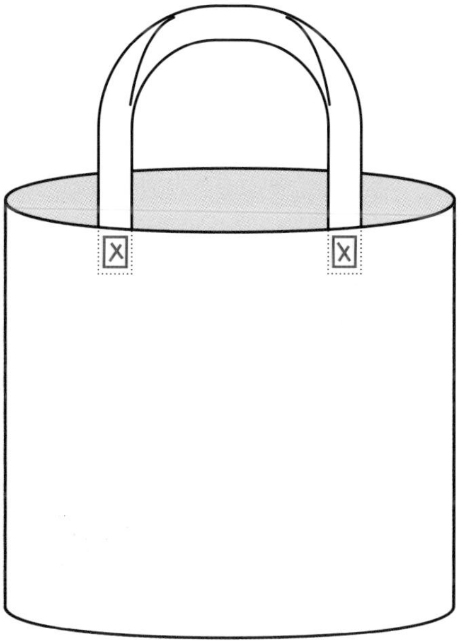

SIPALU BAG

by Kerin Dimeler-Laurence

FINISHED MEASUREMENTS
10.5″ width × 2″ depth × 12″ height;
25″ strap

YARN
Knit Picks Palette™ (fingering weight, 100% Peruvian Highland Wool; 231 yards /50g): Sagebrush 25549, Opal Heather 25096, Seafaring 26048, Spruce 25535, Shoal 26054, Douglas Fir 26046, Lichen 26047, Coriander 25544, Wheat Heather 26056, Thicket 25085, Grizzly Heather 25532, 1 ball each, to make both bags

NEEDLES
US 2 (2.75mm) 32″ and 16″ circular needles and DPNs, or size to obtain gauge
US 3 (3.25mm) DPNs, for I-Cord straps

NOTIONS
Yarn Needle
Stitch Markers
Scrap Yarn
Stitch Holders or more Scrap Yarn
Fabric for Lining
Sewing Thread to match yarn
Sewing Needle
Large Button for closure

GAUGE
32 sts and 32 rows = 4″ in Stranded Stockinette Stitch worked flat and in the round, blocked

For pattern support, contact customerservice@knitpicks.com

Sipalu Bag

Notes:

Inspired by brightly colored Nepalese and Indian textiles, this bag incorporates eleven harmonious colors. The yarn requirements make both included color order versions (same colors, used in a different order). When colors are specified in the text, they are listed as Main Color Order (Alternative Color Order).

Because of the texture on the wrong side of the knitted fabric, it is important that you line the bag. For extra stability, consider using a sew-in interfacing that works well with wool.

When working a chart in the round, read each row from right to left, as a RS row. When working flat, read RS rows from right to left, and WS rows from left to right.

Any sew-in purse handles can be used for this bag in place of knitted handles. Attach them between the knitted fabric and the lining.

DIRECTIONS

Side Panel

Using scrap yarn and a Provisional Cast On, CO 240 sts.
Setup Row (WS): P across with Sagebrush (Douglas Fir), PMs after 80 and 160 sts. Do not join to work in the rnd (Side Panel is worked flat).
Rows 1-17: Work from Side Panel chart, repeating the 12 sts 20 times.
Next Row (WS): P across with Sagebrush (Douglas Fir).

Front & Back of Bag

Side Welt

Row 1 (RS): Switch to Douglas Fir (Sagebrush), K across.
Rows 2-6: Work Rev St st.
Row 7 (RS): With spare needle, PU 240 sts from first row of Douglas Fir (Sagebrush) on WS of work; with RS facing, hold picked up sts behind working sts, knit 1 st from front needle tog with 1 st from back needle; cont across row until all sts have been worked. This creates a lengthwise tube of fabric across your work. 240 sts.
Row 8: P across.

Front of Bag

Provisionally CO 80 sts on spare needle; set aside.
Rnd 1: Using Sagebrush (Douglas Fir) and longer circular needles, begin working from Front Panel chart, repeating chart sts three times across all sts; at end of these reps, PM and cont chart across the 80 CO sts from spare needle. PM and join to work in the rnd. 320 sts.
Rnds 2-40: Cont working from chart through all rnds, changing to shorter circulars and/or DPNs as needed. 8 sts.
Next Rnd: K2tog to end. 4 sts. Break yarn, pass through remaining sts, and pull tight to close.

Back of Bag

Unravel Provisional CO from Side Panel. With RS facing, work Back same as Front, starting from Side Welt directions.

Top Border

PU 80 sts from Provisional CO on Front of bag, 16 sts from Side Panel edge, 80 sts from Back, and 16 sts from other side; PM and join to work in the rnd. 192 sts.

Lower Top Welt

Rnd 1: With Douglas Fir (Sagebrush), K all.
Rnds 2-6: P all.
Finish welt as for Side Welts.

Work Top Border chart, repeating the 12 sts 16 times around.

Upper Top Welt

Work same as Lower Top Welt, through Rnd 6. On final (joining) rnd, instead of leaving live sts, work sts loosely and pass 1 st over the next as in a 3-Needle Bind Off.

Straps

With US 3 (3.25mm) DPN, PU 6 sts along BO edge of Upper Top Welt at corner 1 of bag (see diagram). With Coriander Heather and Shoal (Opal Heather and Grizzly Heather) held tog as one, work 2 rows in St st, then work as I-Cord for 3″. Put sts on st holder or scrap yarn and break yarn.
Rep at corner 2, but leave sts on needle and do not break yarn. Place sts from holder onto needle, to the right of live I-Cord sts. 12 sts. Work all 12 sts as I-Cord (distribute on more than one DPN if necessary) for two rnds.
Next Rnd: K2tog around. 6 sts.
Work as 6-st I-Cord for 20″. Break yarn and put sts on holder.

Rep at other corners; working first in corner 3 then corner 4. Graft live ends of I-Cord strap tog.

Button Loop

With Coriander Heather and Shoal (Opal Heather and Grizzly Heather) held tog as one, PU 6 sts from WS of BO edge so that leftmost st is 0.5″ to the right of the center Back.
Work as I-Cord for 8″.
Sew live sts down so that rightmost st is 1″ to the left of the picked up sts.

Finishing

For body, tie yarn ends tog (or braid) tightly. There is no need to weave in most ends, as the lining will hide them.

Weave in any remaining visible ends, wash, and block. You may find it helpful to block the finished bag over a stack of books or a cardboard box (cover books or box with plastic wrap or a plastic bag first).

Sew large decorative button 1″ down from top edge, in center of Top Border band.
Sew in lining, and interfacing if desired.

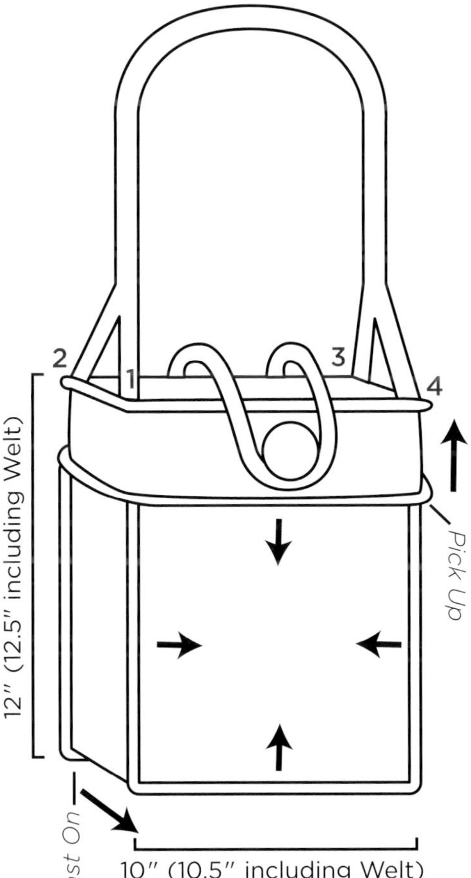

Bag is knit in the direction of the arrows.

Front Panel—Main Color Order

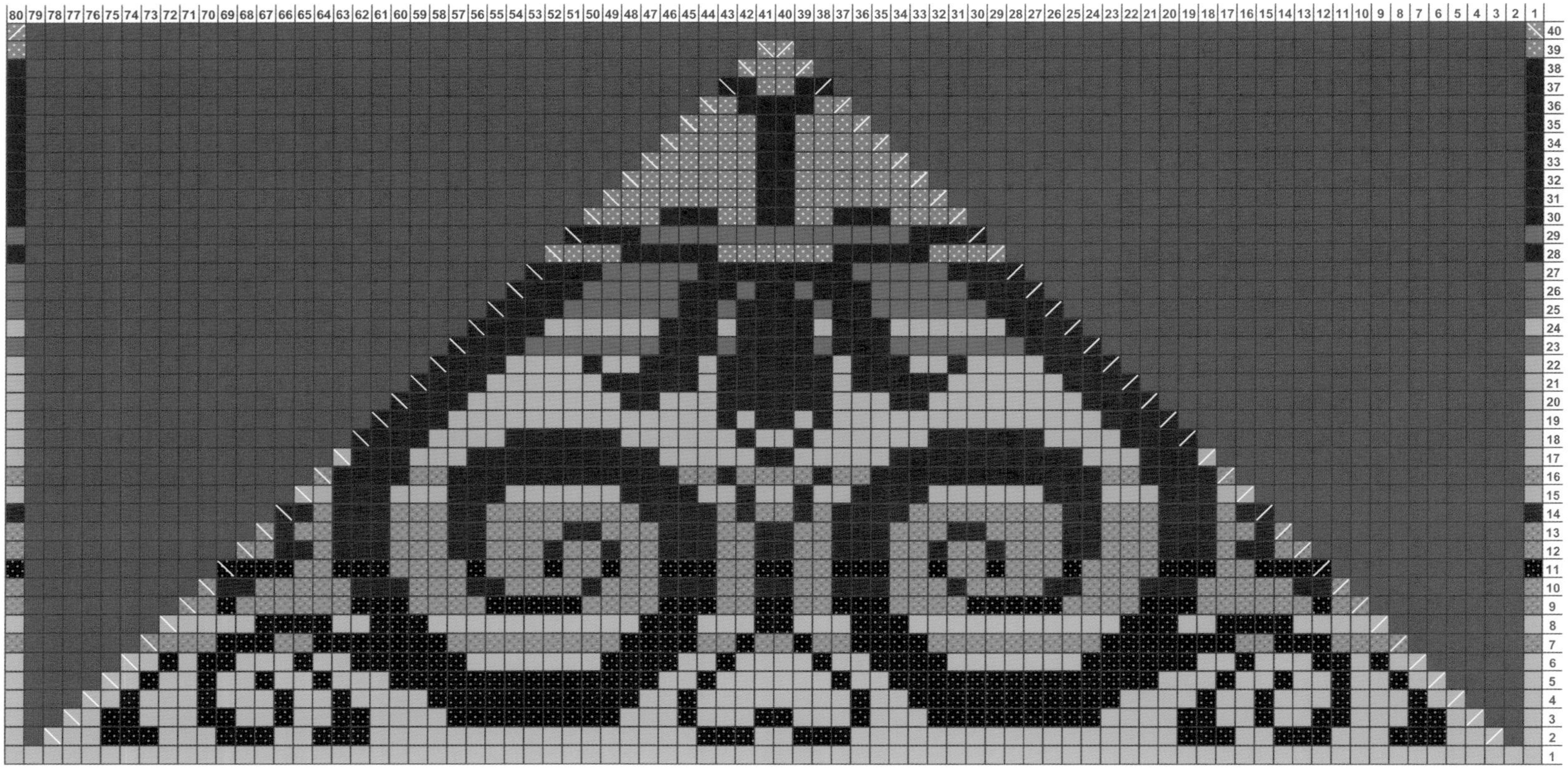

Side Panel—Main

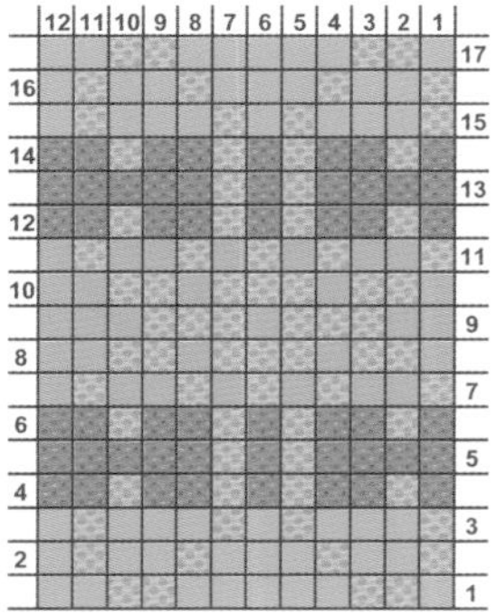

Top Border—Main

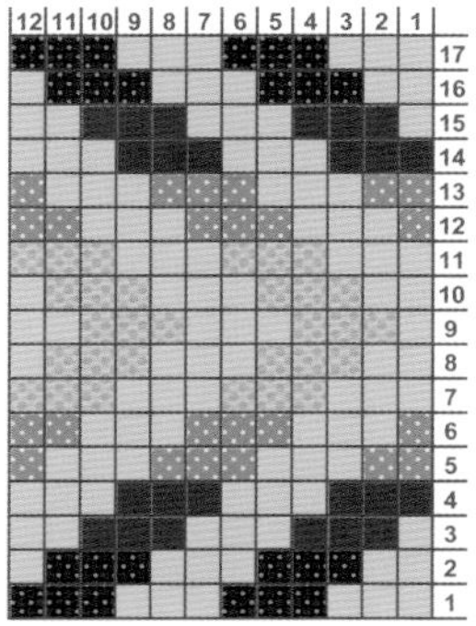

LEGEND

- Sagebrush
- Opal Heather
- Seafaring
- Spruce
- Shoal
- Douglas Fir
- Lichen
- Coriander Heather
- Wheat Heather
- Thicket
- Grizzly Heather
- **No Stitch** Placeholder—no stitch made
- **Knit Stitch**
- **K2tog** Knit 2 stitches together as one stitch
- **SSK** Slip, slip, knit slipped stitches together

Front Panel—Alternative Color Order

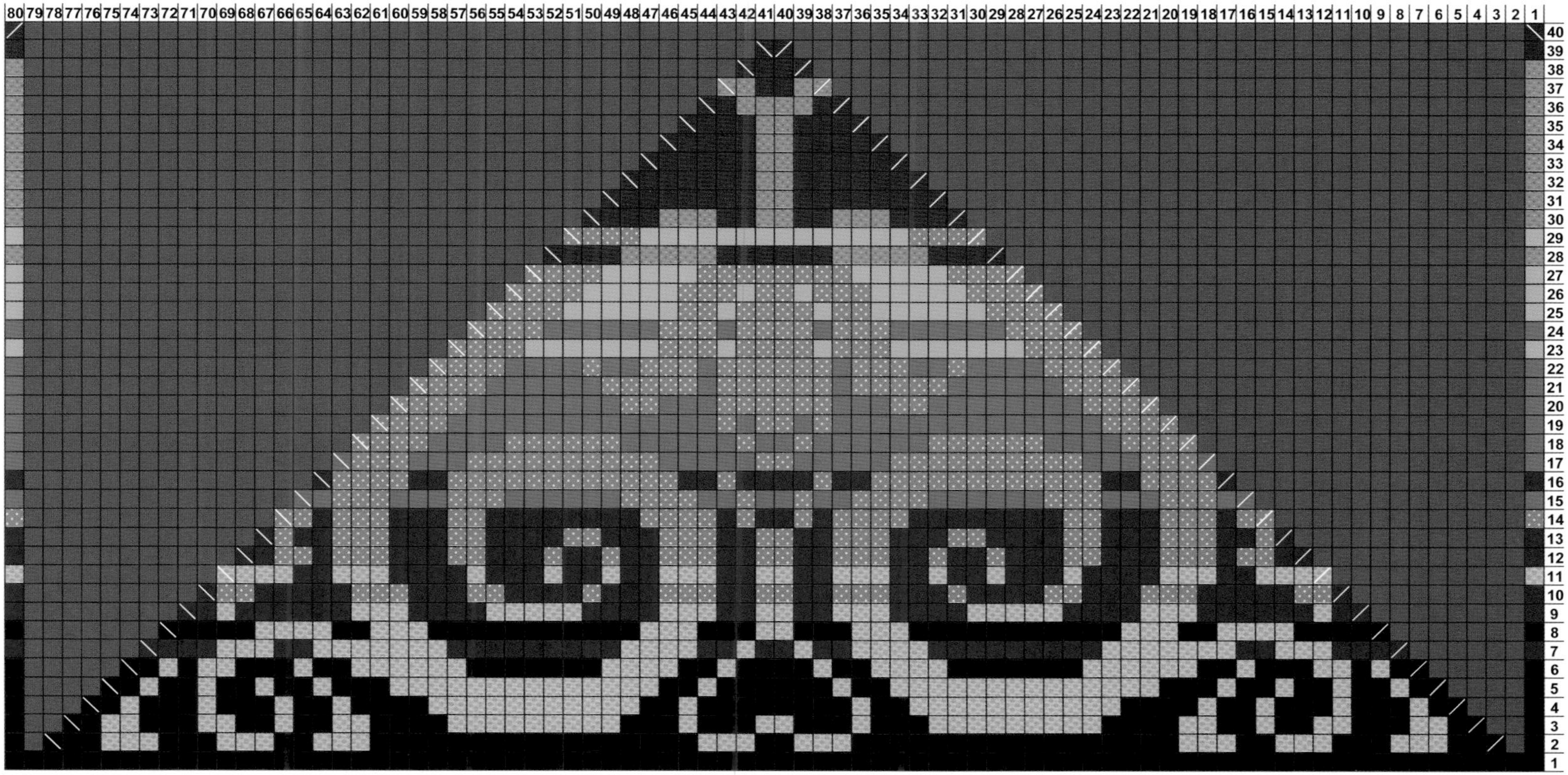

Side Panel—Alternative

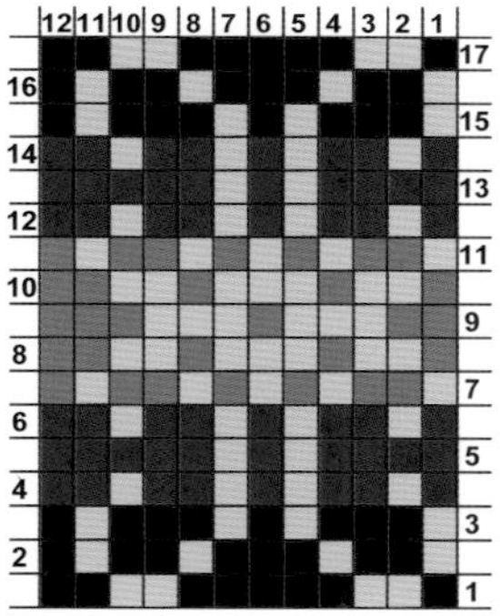

Top Border—Alternative

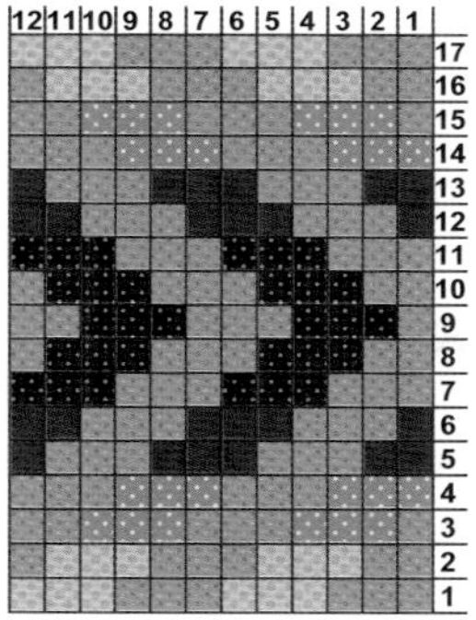

LEGEND

- Sagebrush
- Opal Heather
- Seafaring
- Spruce
- Shoal
- Douglas Fir
- Lichen
- Coriander Heather
- Wheat Heather
- Thicket
- Grizzly Heather
- **No Stitch** Placeholder—no stitch made
- **Knit Stitch**
- **K2tog** Knit 2 stitches together as one stitch
- **SSK** Slip, slip, knit slipped stitches together

TERNION KNEE SOCKS

by Kerin Dimeler-Laurence

FINISHED MEASUREMENTS

Approximately 8″ foot circumference, to fit Women's Medium

YARN

Knit Picks Stroll™ (fingering weight, 75% Superwash Merino wool, 25% Nylon; 231 yards/50g)
Lace: White 26082 *or* Black 23701, 4 balls
Cabled: Dove Heather 25023 *or* Wonderland Heather 25028, 4 balls
Argyle: MC Dove Heather 25023, 3 balls; C1 White 26082, C2 Rainforest Heather 25608, 1 ball each *or* MC Grizzly Heather 27238, 3 balls; C1 Dove Heather 25023, C2 Dogwood Heather 25603, 1 ball each

NEEDLES

US 1 (2.25mm) DPNs, and two 24″ circular needles for two circulars technique or 32″ or longer circular needles for Magic Loop technique, or size to obtain gauge

US 2 (2.75mm) DPNs, and two 24″ circular needles for two circulars technique or 32″ or longer circular needles for Magic Loop technique, or size to obtain gauge

NOTIONS

Yarn Needle
Stitch Markers
Cable Needle, for Cabled Socks only

GAUGE

30 sts and 40 rnds = 4″ in Lace Pattern in the round on smaller needles, blocked
32 sts and 40 rows = 4″ in Argyle Pattern on larger needles, blocked
36 sts and 40 rnds = 4″ in Cabled Pattern in the round on larger needles, blocked

For pattern support, contact customerservice@knitpicks.com

Ternion Knee Socks

Notes:

This set of three pairs of knee-high socks has a little something for every occasion: stately argyle, classic cables, or alluring lace will complement any outfit.

Each pair is knit toe up with a gusset heel, and the patterns are written for knitting both socks at once, eliminating the chance of second sock syndrome. Also, this two-at-a-time, toe-up construction allows you to use as much yarn as you have with no risk of running out, making socks as long as you like!

Decide which pattern you will make, and determine needle and yarn needed, then read your chosen pattern before starting to work from the General Directions.

When working a chart in the round, read each row from right to left, as a RS row. When working flat, read RS rows from right to left, and WS rows from left to right.

M1L-P (make 1 left-leaning stitch purl-wise)
PU bar between st just worked and next st, and place on LH needle mounted as a regular knit st; purl through back loop.

M1R-P (make 1 right-leaning stitch purl-wise)
PU bar between st just worked and next st, and place on LH needle backwards (twisted st mount); purl through front.

GENERAL DIRECTIONS

Toes

Work CO steps using spare DPNs, then transfer to circular needles when the pattern instructs you to.
Using the Backward Loop Cast On, CO 8 sts for a narrow toe, 10 sts for average, or 12 sts for a wider toe.
Knit across these sts.
Turning work so that CO edge is on top and working yarn is to the right of the work, PU and K into each CO st (including slip knot).
You are now working in the rnd; the first 8 (10, 12) sts are the Instep, the second are the Sole.

On a second pair of DPNs, CO for second sock in the same way using a second ball of yarn.
Transfer first sock to two (or one if using Magic Loop) circular needles by knitting the first Inc Round (below) directly off the DPNs. On two circulars, the Instep will be on one needle and Sole sts on the other.

Inc Rnd: K1, M1L, K to last st of Instep, M1R, K1; rep for Sole sts. 4 sts inc.
Now, transfer the second sock in the same way, to work both socks at once. Rep directions around both socks.
Work St st, repeating Inc Round every rnd two more times, then every other rnd, until each sock has 60 sts for Lace and Argyle Socks, and 64 sts for Cabled Socks.
Consider the first 30 (32) sts of the rnd to be the Instep, and the second 30 (32) sts to be the Sole. Extra sts will be added to accommodate the drawing-in of the cables.

Skip ahead to follow directions for sock pattern of your choice and work to 3" from the back of your heel, then begin working Gusset Heel, as follows, over heel sts.

Gusset Heel

This heel is a standard gusset and flap style heel, but worked from the toe up. St counts are given for 60 sts (68 sts for Cabled Sock).
Gusset Setup: Work across Instep sts in pattern; across Sole sts: K1, M1L, K14 (15), PM, K14 (15), M1R, K1. 2 sts inc. 32 (34) sts across heel.
Knit one rnd, maintaining pattern on Instep.

Inc Rnd: Work across Instep sts in pattern; across Sole sts: K1, M1L, K to last st, M1R, K1. 2 sts inc.
Next Rnd: K all, maintaining pattern on Instep.
Rep these two rnds nine more times. 52 (54) sts across heel.

First Short Row Segment
If knitting two socks at a time, work each short row section individually. Work first sock to **, then rep from * to ** for second sock. Resume knitting two-at-a-time once all short row sections are complete.

***Short Row 1 (RS):** Work across Instep in pattern, then across heel to 9 sts past M; M1R, K1, W&T.
Short Row 2 (WS): P to 9 sts past M, M1L-P, P1, W&T.
Short Row 3: K to 7 sts past M, M1R, K1, W&T.
Short Row 4: P to 7 sts past M, M1L-P, P1, W&T.
Short Row 5: K to 5 sts past M, M1R, K1, W&T.
Short Row 6: P to 5 sts past M, M1L-P, P1, W&T.
58 (60) sts across heel.

Second Short Row Segment
Setup Row (RS): Knit across heel, picking up wraps and working them tog with the sts they wrap; work across Instep in pattern, then to 14 (15) sts past M on heel, picking up wraps and working them tog with the sts they wrap and removing M; SSK, turn. 57 (59) heel sts.

Short Row 1 (WS): Sl1, P28 (30), P2tog, turn. 1 st dec.
Short Row 2 (RS): Sl1, (Sl1, K1) 14 (15) times, SSK, turn. 1 st dec.
Short Row 3: Rep Short Row 1.
Short Row 4: Sl1, (K1, Sl1) 14 (15) times, SSK, turn. 1 st dec.
Rep Short Rows 1-4 until there are 30 (32) sts remaining on heel side, having worked a WS row last.**
Begin working in the rnd, continuing on using the pattern for your chosen socks.

Lace Instep

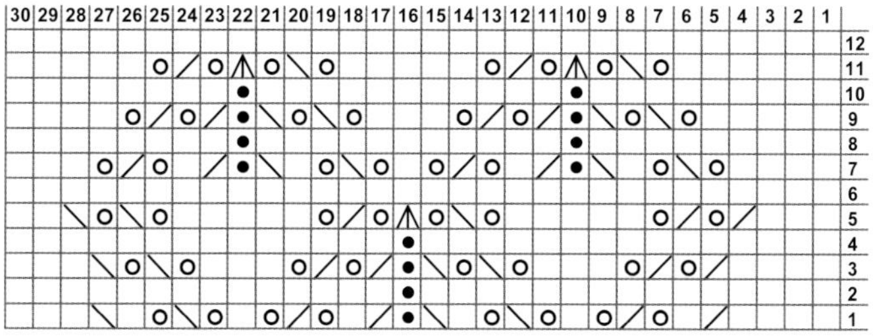

Lace Pattern

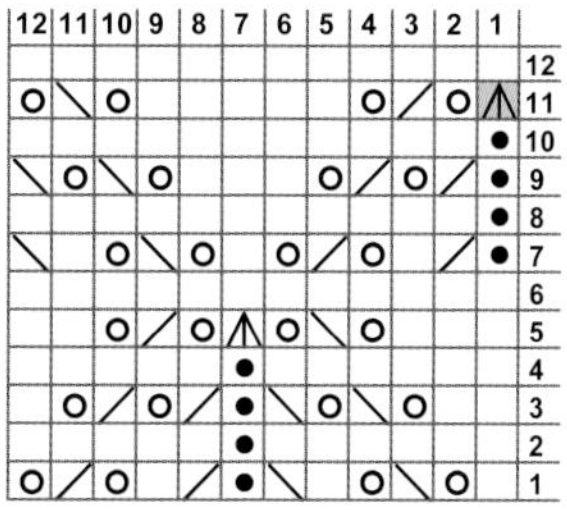

Lace Gusset

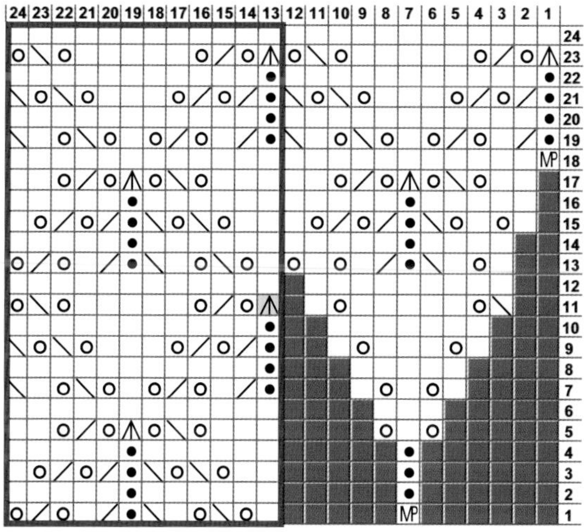

Rep five times

Note: On first rep, work St 13 in Row 11 as a K2tog

LEGEND

No Stitch
Placeholder—no stitch made

Knit Stitch

Purl Stitch

YO
Yarn over

K2tog
Knit 2 stitches together as one stitch

SSK
Slip, slip, knit slipped stitches together

CDD
Slip first and second stitches together as if to K2tog; knit 1 stitch; pass 2 slipped stitches over the knit stitch

CDD across rounds (work at start of new round)
Slip last st of previous round onto left-hand needle, slip first and second stitches together as if to K2tog; knit 1 stitch; pass 2 slipped stitches over the knit stitch

M1P
Make 1 purl stitch

Pattern Repeat

LACE DIRECTIONS

CO for Toes using smaller needles, and follow Toes directions; once toes are complete, begin working Lace Instep chart across Instep sts, working the Sole in St st. Work to 3" before the back of your heel, working reps of Lace Instep chart over Instep sts only.

Work Gusset Heel as instructed. Once heel is complete, work around leg to last rnd of current rep of Lace Instep chart. Work across Instep in pattern over the last rnd, then through 15 sts of heel side, PM for new BOR.

Work Lace Pattern chart, repeating chart sts five times around. Work five reps of the 12 rnds of chart.

Lace Socks Leg Gusset
Work Lace Gusset chart Rnds 1-24. 72 sts.

Work Lace Pattern chart again, repeating chart sts six times around. Work three reps of the 12 rnds of chart.

Ribbing
Rnd 1: K all.
Work 2x2 Rib for 2" or desired length.
BO using a Stretchy Bind Off of your choice.

Finishing
Weave in ends, wash, block, and enjoy!

ARGYLE DIRECTIONS

These are worked in plain St st over the foot. They can be knit two-at-a-time up until the Gusset Heel; work the intarsia chart portions one sock at a time. Because there are so many ends in intarsia, weave them in as you go to save time later.

Make several small balls or butterflies each of Dove Heather, White, and Rainforest Heather.

CO for Toes in Dove Heather, using larger needles, and follow Toes directions. Cont to knit foot in St st, to 3" before the back of your heel. Work to end of Gusset Heel directions.

Knit one rnd, then K 15 sts of the heel side. This is the back of sock and is the beginning of row for intarsia portion. Every row of intarsia portion is charted, worked back and forth.

Turn work and begin working from Argyle Chart on WS Row 1, attaching a new ball of yarn for each section of color. The single-st diagonal lines can each be worked from one ball.

Row 41 marks beginning of gusset. Work through Row 120. Break all attached yarn except for last section of Basalt Heather.

LEGEND

- **No Stitch** Placeholder—no stitch made
- **Main Color (Dove Heather)**
- **Contrasting Color 1 (White)**
- **Contrasting Color 2 (Rainforest Heather)**
- **Knit Stitch**
- MR **M1R-P (worked on WS)** Make 1 right-leaning purl stitch
- ML **M1L-P (worked on WS)** Make 1 left-leaning purl stitch
- **Pattern Repeat**

Argyle Chart

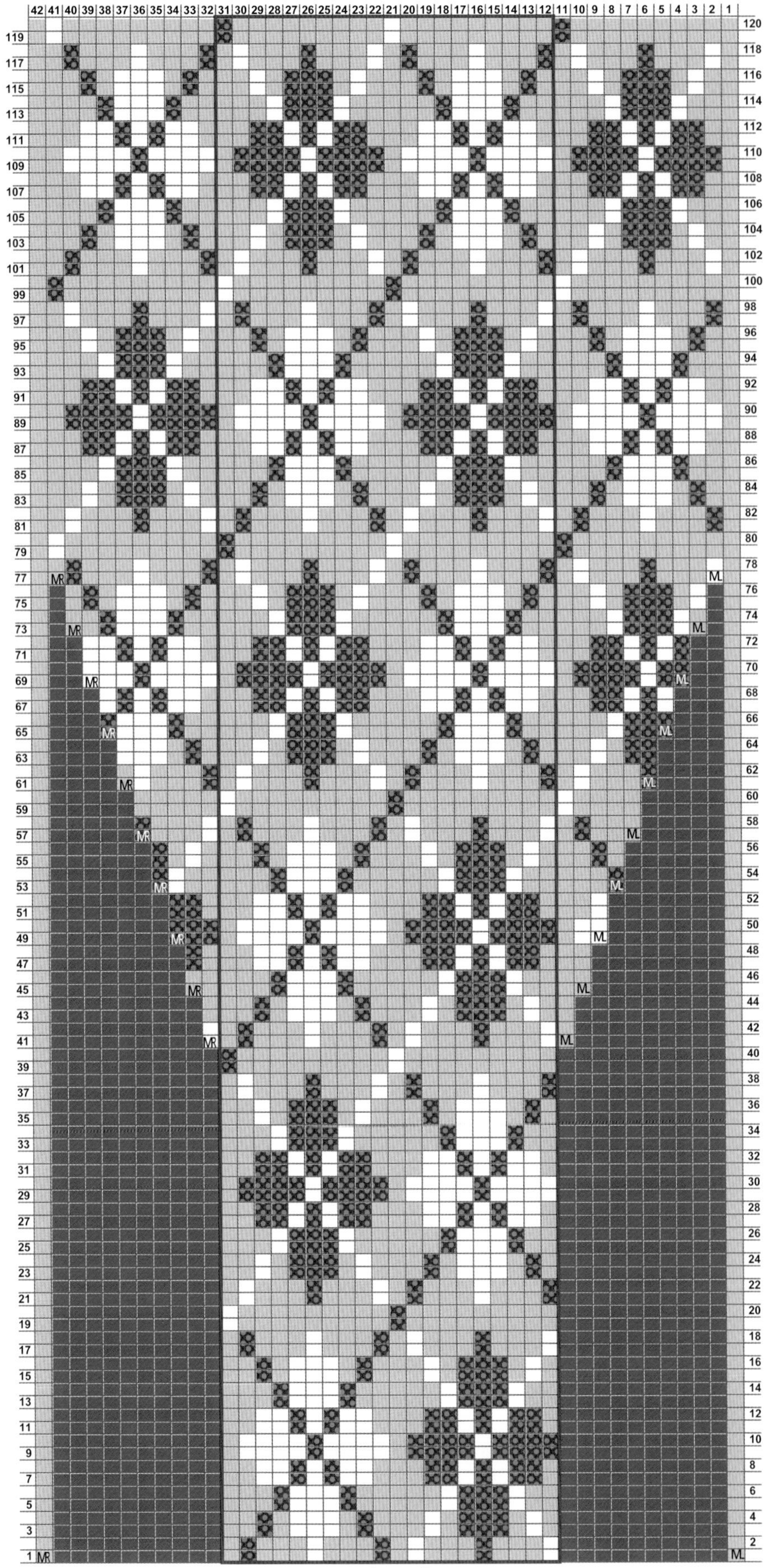

Rep three times

Next Row: K2tog, K to last 2 sts of rnd, SSK. 80 sts.
PM and join back in the rnd.

Ribbing

Setup Rnd: *(K2, P2) three times, K2tog, K1, P2, K2, P2; rep from * three more times, ending the last rep before the final K2, P2. 76 sts.
Work 2x2 Rib for 2" or desired length.
BO using a Stretchy Bind Off of your choice.

Finishing

Weave in ends and carefully sew leg seam, matching pattern.
Wash, block, and enjoy!

CABLED DIRECTIONS

CO for Toes using larger needles, and follow Toes directions; once toes are complete, work a setup rnd for Instep: *(K2, PFB, K2, P2) two times, K2; rep from * once more across Instep (36 sts on Instep), work across heel sts in St st.

Begin working from Cable Chart across Instep on next rnd (red boxed sts make up the Instep pattern), keeping Sole in St st, and cont to 3" before the back of your heel.

Work Gusset Heel as instructed. Once heel is complete, work around leg to last rnd of current rep of Cable Chart boxed rep.

LEGEND

No Stitch
Placeholder—no stitch made

Knit Stitch

Purl Stitch

PFB
Purl into the front and back of the stitch

M1R
Make 1 right-leaning stitch

M1L
Make 1 left-leaning stitch

M1P
Make 1 purl stitch

Pattern Repeat

Right Twist (RT)
Sl1 to CN, hold in back; K1, K1 from CN

Left Twist (LT)
Sl1 to CN, hold in front; K1, K1 from CN

Right Twist, Purl back (RPT)
Sl1 to CN, hold in back; K1, P1 from CN

Left Twist, Purl back (LPT)
Sl1 to CN, hold in front; P1, K1 from CN

Cable 2 Over 2 Right (2/2 RC)
Sl2 to CN, hold in back; K2, K2 from CN

Cable 2 Over 2 Left (2/2 LC)
Sl2 to CN, hold in front; K2, K2 from CN

Cable 2 Over 2 Right, Purl back (2/2 RPC)
Sl2 to CN, hold in back; K2, P2 from CN

Cable 2 Over 2 Left, Purl back (2/2 LPC)
Sl2 to CN, hold in front; P2, K2 from CN

Cable Chart

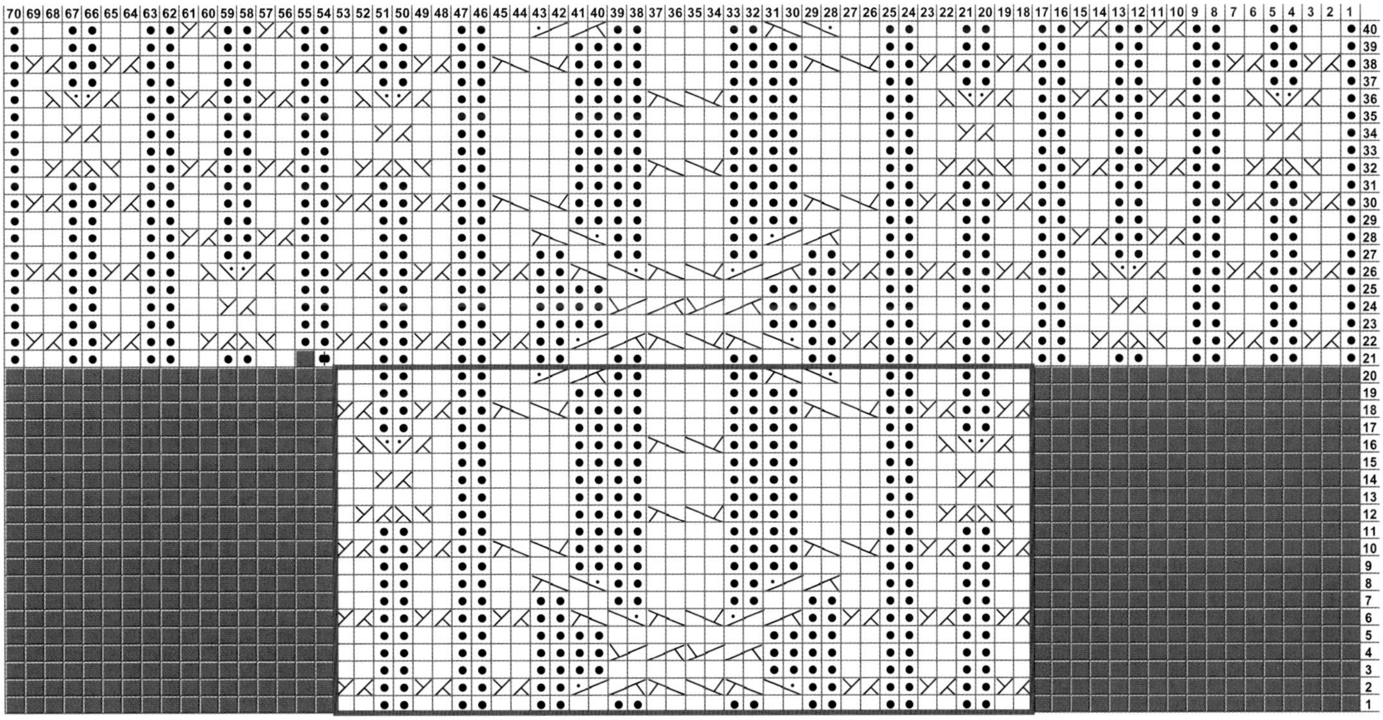

After working Rnd 20 across Instep, set up heel side sts: PFB, (K2, P2) three times, K2, P1, PM for new BOR.

Work Rnd 21 of Cable Chart, working sts 16-17 as PFB to bring total number of sts on heel side to 34.
Cont working from Cable Chart through Rnd 40.
Work one more rep of Rnds 21-40.

Gusset

Work Cable Gusset chart, working incs in gusset as they appear; there are now 78 sts around sock.
Rep Rnds 41-60 until sock measures 11" to obtain desired height of sock.

Ribbing

Setup Rnd: P1, *(K2, P2) ten times, SSK, K2tog, (P2, K2) eight times, P1. 76 sts.
Work 2x2 Rib for 2" or desired length.
BO using a Stretchy Bind Off of your choice.

Finishing

Weave in ends, wash, block, and enjoy!

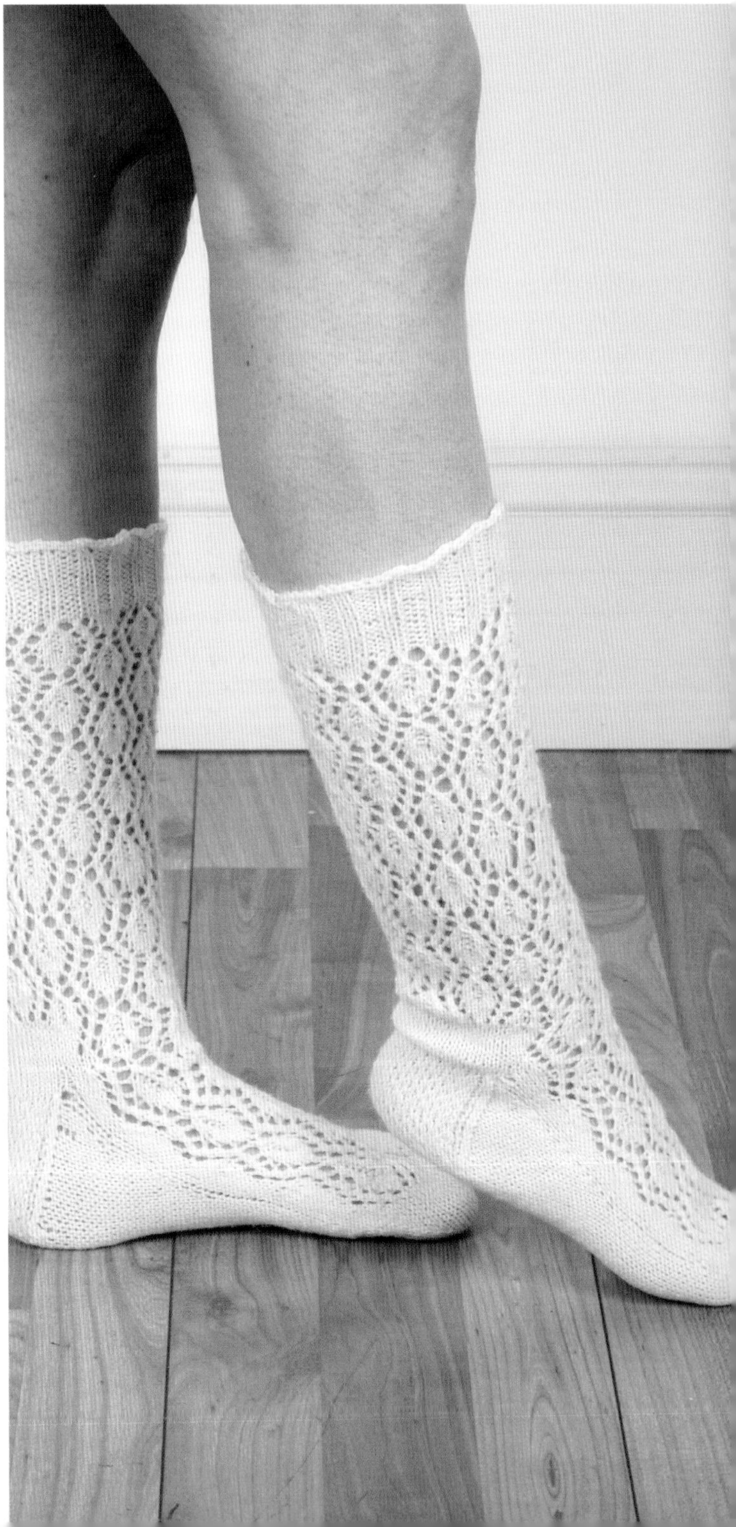

Cable Gusset

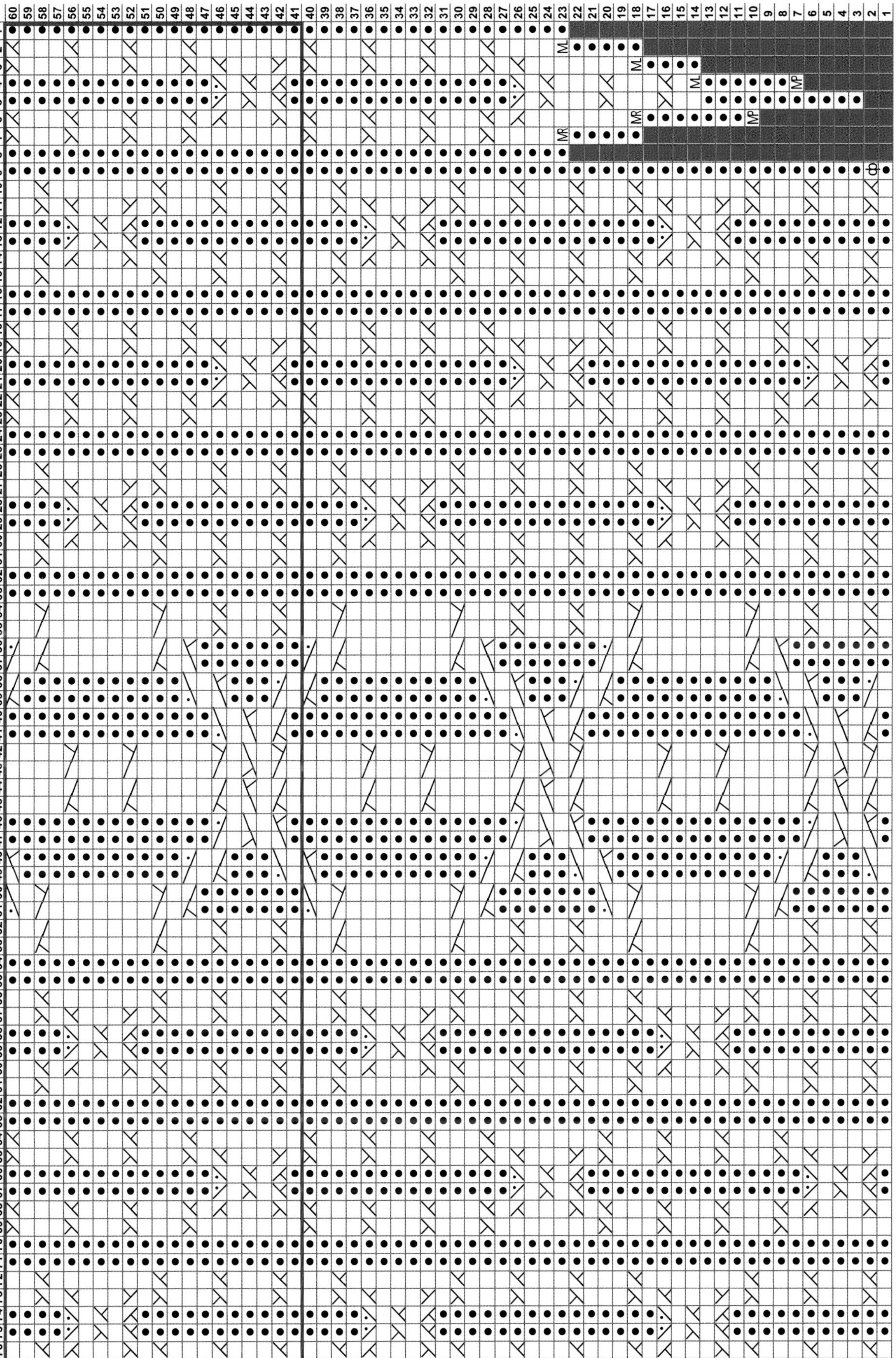

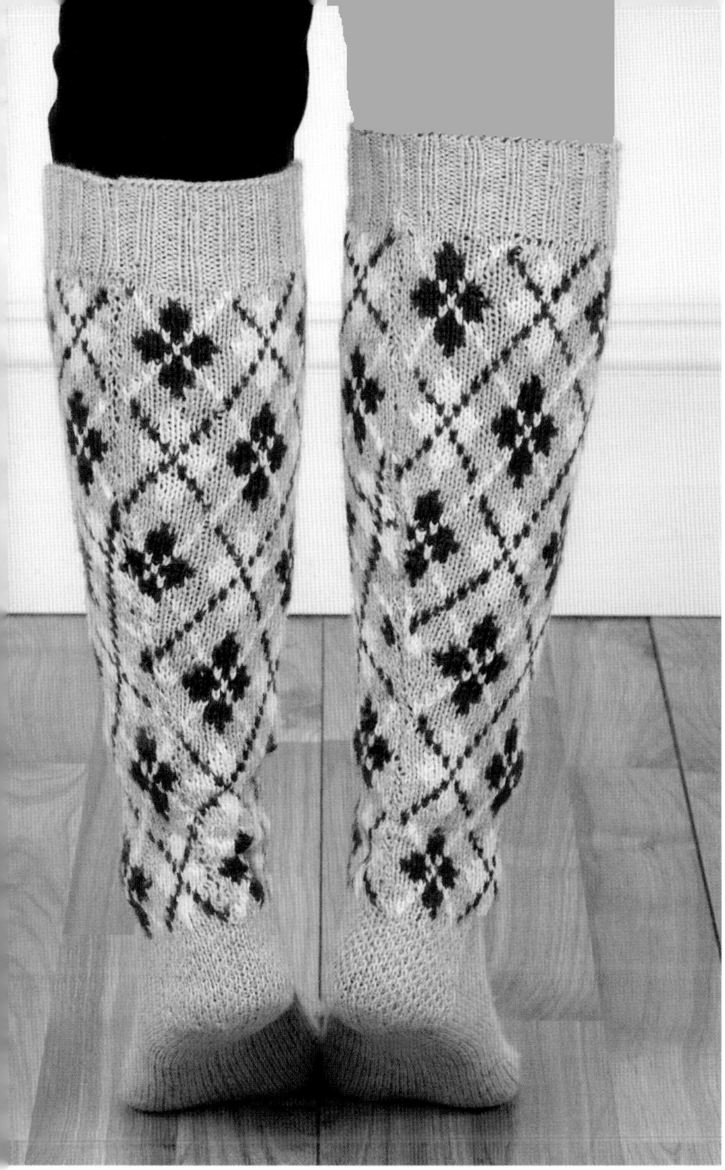

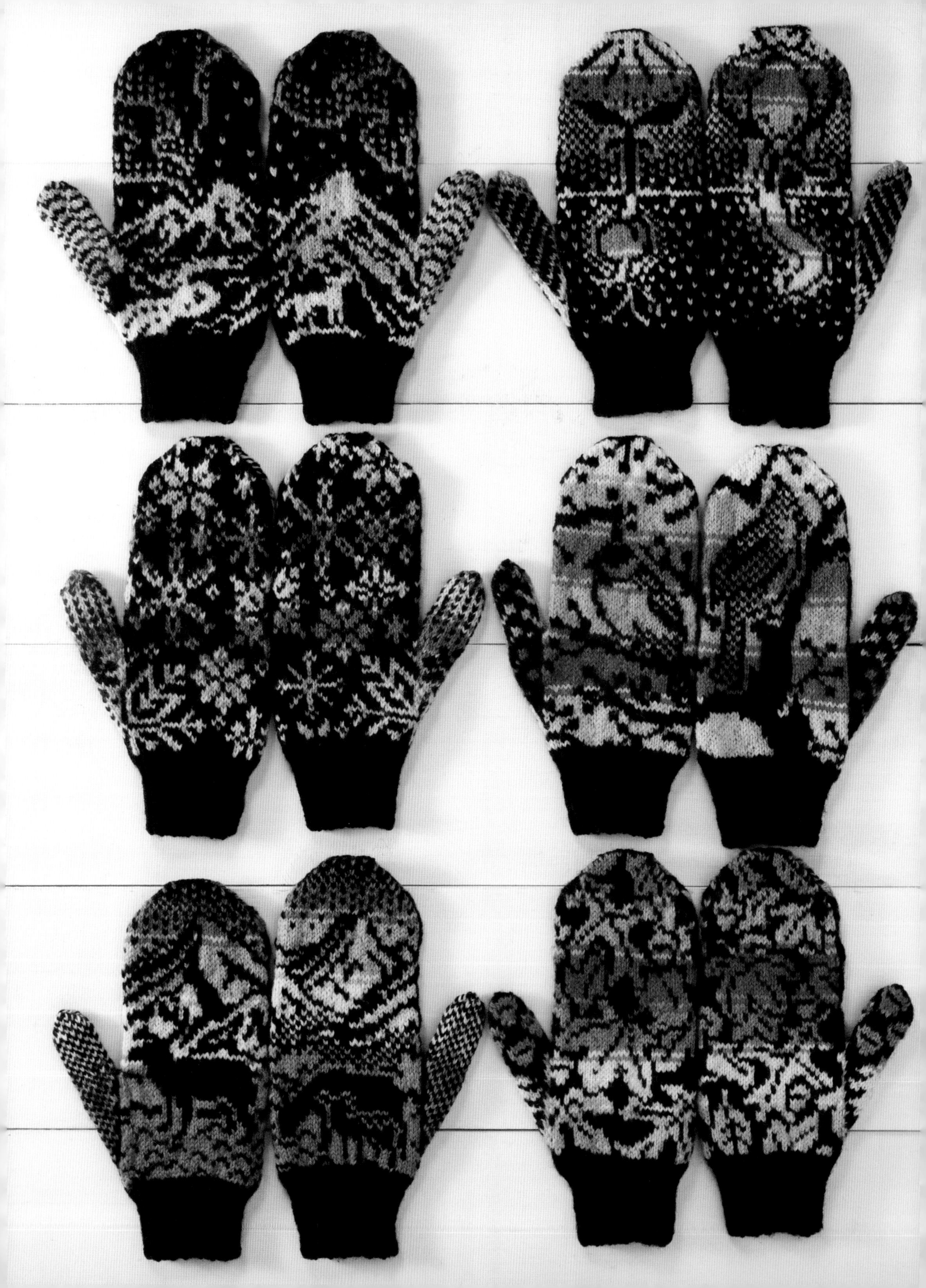

WOODLAND WINTER MITTENS

by Kerin Dimeler-Laurence

FINISHED MEASUREMENTS
8" hand circumference × 10.5 (11)" length, including cuff, to fit Women's S/M (M/L)

YARN
Knit Picks Palette™ (100% Peruvian Highland Wool; 231 yards/50g):
4 balls main color, 1 ball each of ten colors, to make all six pairs of mittens (see chart pages for two colorways)

NEEDLES
US 1 (2.25mm) DPNs or 32" or longer circular needles for Magic Loop technique, or size to obtain gauge

US 0 (2mm) DPNs or 32" or longer circular needles for Magic Loop technique, or one size smaller than size used to obtain gauge

NOTIONS
Yarn Needle
Stitch Markers
Stitch Holder or Scrap Yarn
Spare DPNs

GAUGE
30 sts and 32 rnds = 4" in Stranded Stockinette Stitch in the round, blocked

For pattern support, contact customerservice@knitpicks.com

Woodland Winter Mittens

Notes:

Knit your way through the seasons with the Woodland Winter Mitts! These stranded colorwork mitts are sure to keep your hands toasty warm as you knit a pair for every month from October to March. The scene on each pair of mitts shows off the transitions of winter, starting with falling leaves, then grazing elk, northern lights, snowflakes, snow birds, and finally a sprouting seed. Each mitten has a different picture on each hand, which creates a larger scene when you hold your hands together.

All twelve of the mittens begin with simple ribbing, which can be adjusted for length to suit your hands and preference. The palm circumference can easily be adjusted by changing needle size; a stitch gauge of 32 stitches per 4" results in a 7.5" circumference, a gauge of 28 stitches makes 8.5", and a gauge of 25 stitches makes 9.5". Be careful not to pull the floats tightly across the wrong side of the work—stranded Stockinette Stitch is not very stretchy and this will result in a too-snug mitten!

The charts are worked in the round; read each row from right to left, as a RS row.

Work around all stitches of the thumb following the chart for the correct hand and size, noting that some mittens have different thumb charts for each hand.

DIRECTIONS

Cuff

With MC, CO 56 (60) sts onto smaller needles. PM and join in the rnd, being careful not to twist sts.
Work 2x2 Rib for 2" or as long as you prefer.

Hand

Switch to larger needles.
Size S/M, Next Rnd: (K14, M1) four times. 60 sts.
Size M/L, Next Rnd: K all.

Work from either Left or Right Hand chart of any pair of mittens. All incs, color changes, and thumb gusset sts are shown in the chart.
PMs for thumb gusset before and after first inc st on Rnd 5 of chart.
On Rnd 25, knit to first gusset M, remove M and place 20 thumb sts on st holder or scrap yarn. Remove second M and cont with next live st of Rnd 25.

After last rnd of chart, place one half of sts on one needle and one half on another (or two ends of a circular needle). With MC, graft the two sides tog using Kitchener Stitch.

Thumb

Place 20 held thumb sts onto larger needles. Attach yarn with rnd beginning in thumb crotch.
Begin knitting from Rnd 1 of Thumb chart for your chosen mitten, then PM and join the rnd.
Cont following Thumb chart to last rnd.
Break yarn, leaving a 6" tail of MC. With a yarn needle, pass this tail through remaining live sts and pull tight to close hole.

Second Mitten

Work second mitt of the pair from the other chart.

Finishing

Weave in ends (color change ends can be tied together inside mitten instead of woven in). Use tails from beginning of thumb to close any holes in thumb crotch. Wash and block.

LEGEND: STORMY COLORWAY

- Clarity
- Sagebrush
- Opal Heather
- Tarragon
- Celadon Heather
- Serpentine
- Mist
- Suede
- Cream
- Finnley Heather
- Black
- **No Stitch** Placeholder—no stitch made
- Knit Stitch
- **M1R** Make 1 right-leaning stitch
- **M1L** Make 1 left-leaning stitch
- **K2tog** Knit 2 stitches together as one stitch
- **SSK** Slip, slip, knit slipped stitches together
- Size S/M Decreases
- Size M/L Decreases

STORMY COLORWAY

4 balls:
MC Black 23729

1 ball each:
Clarity 25548
Sagebrush 25549
Opal Heather 25096
Tarragon 25099
Celadon Heather 24254
Serpentine 25100
Mist 23733
Suede 24242
Cream 23730
Finnley Heather 26043

All Thumb Charts

October—Both Hands

November—Right Hand

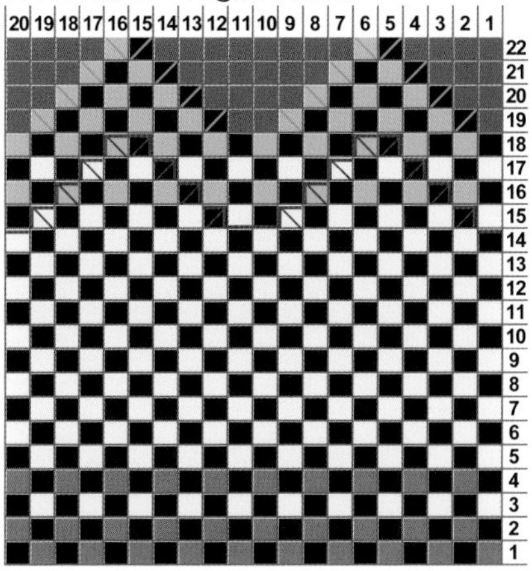

November—Left Hand

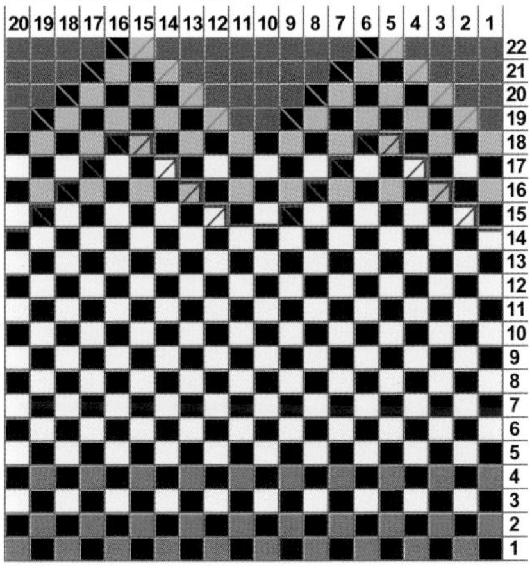

December—Both Hands

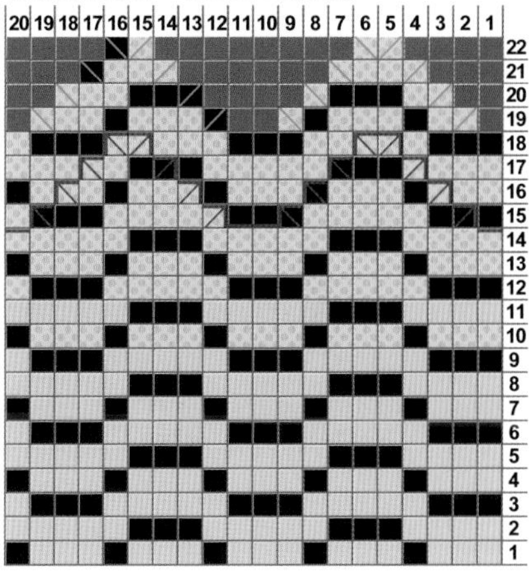

January—Both Hands

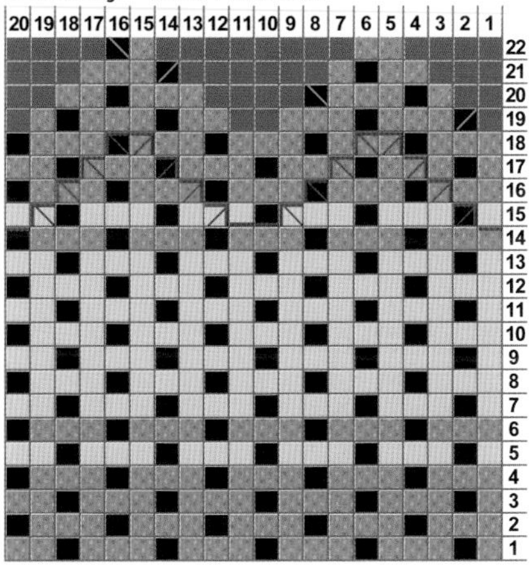

February—Right Hand

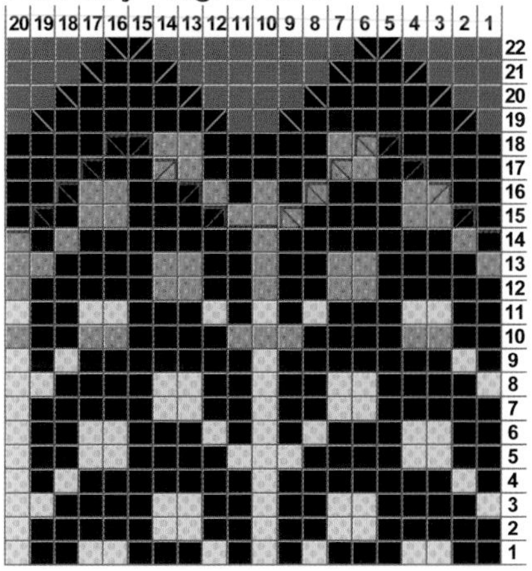

February—Left Hand

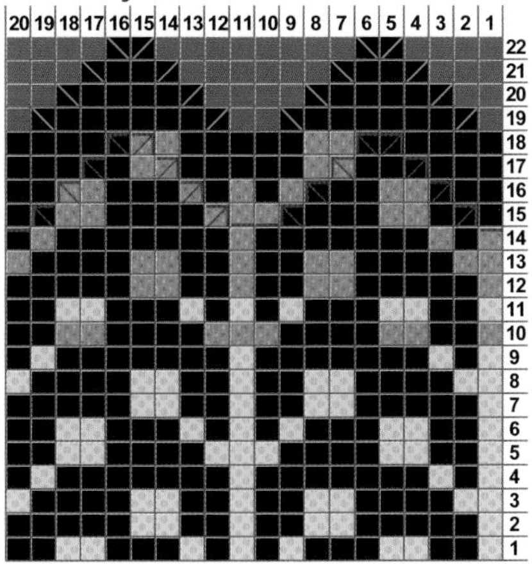

March—Both Hands

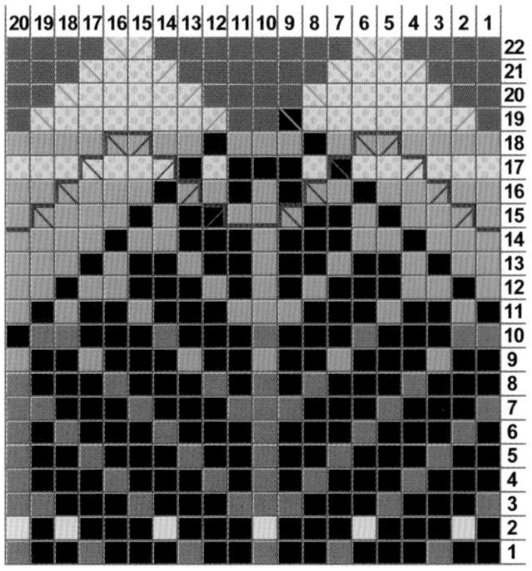

October—Left

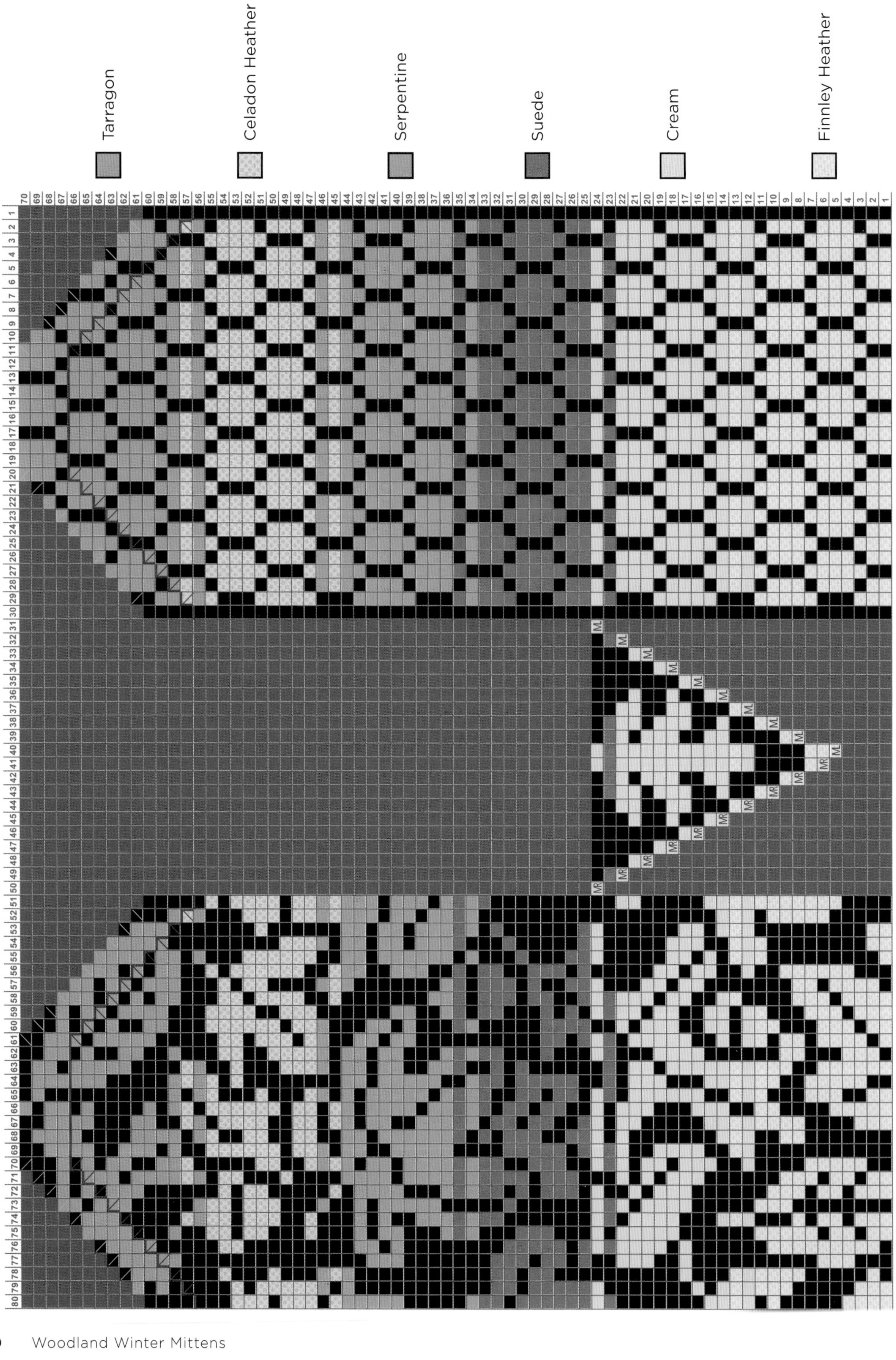

October—Right

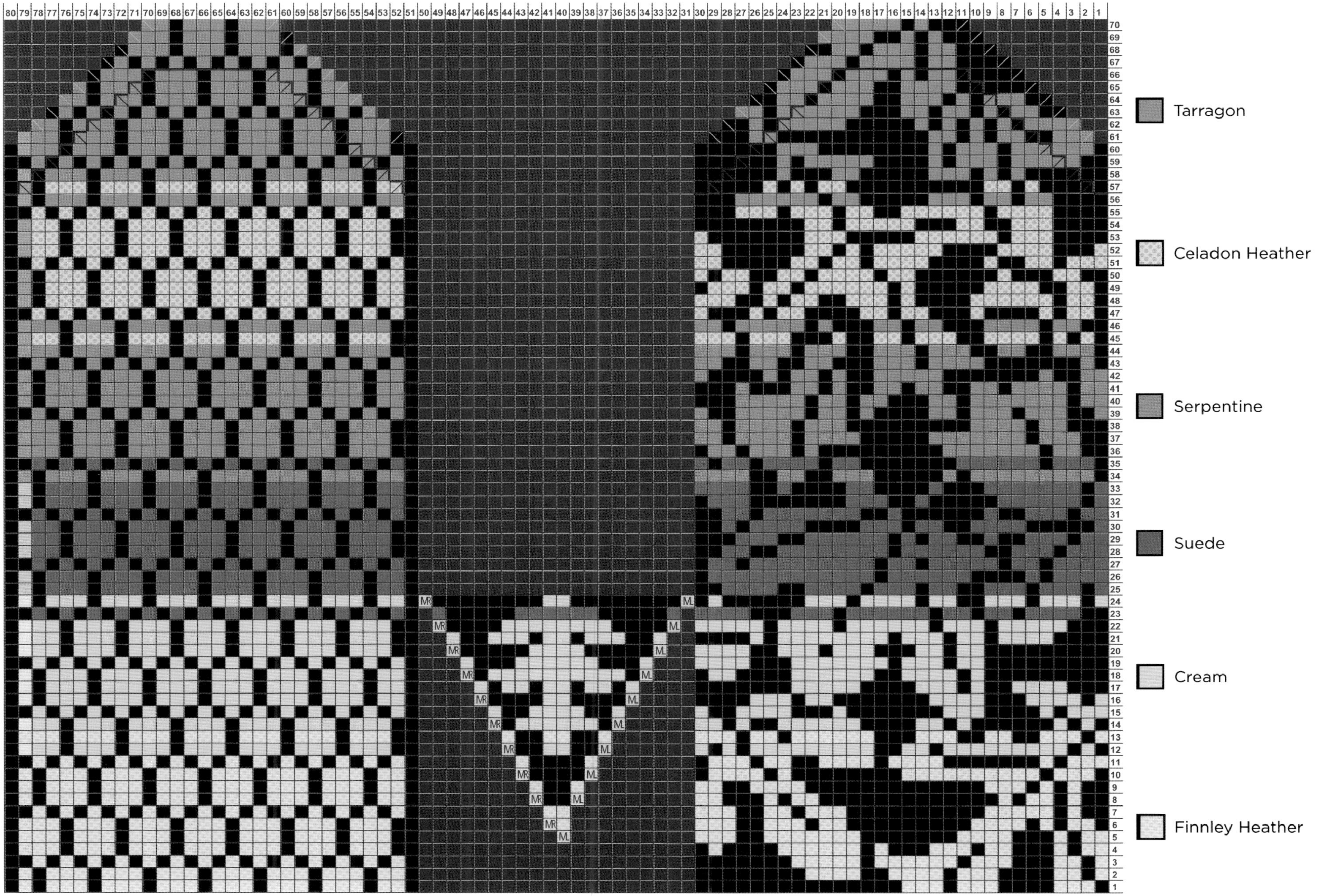

November—Left

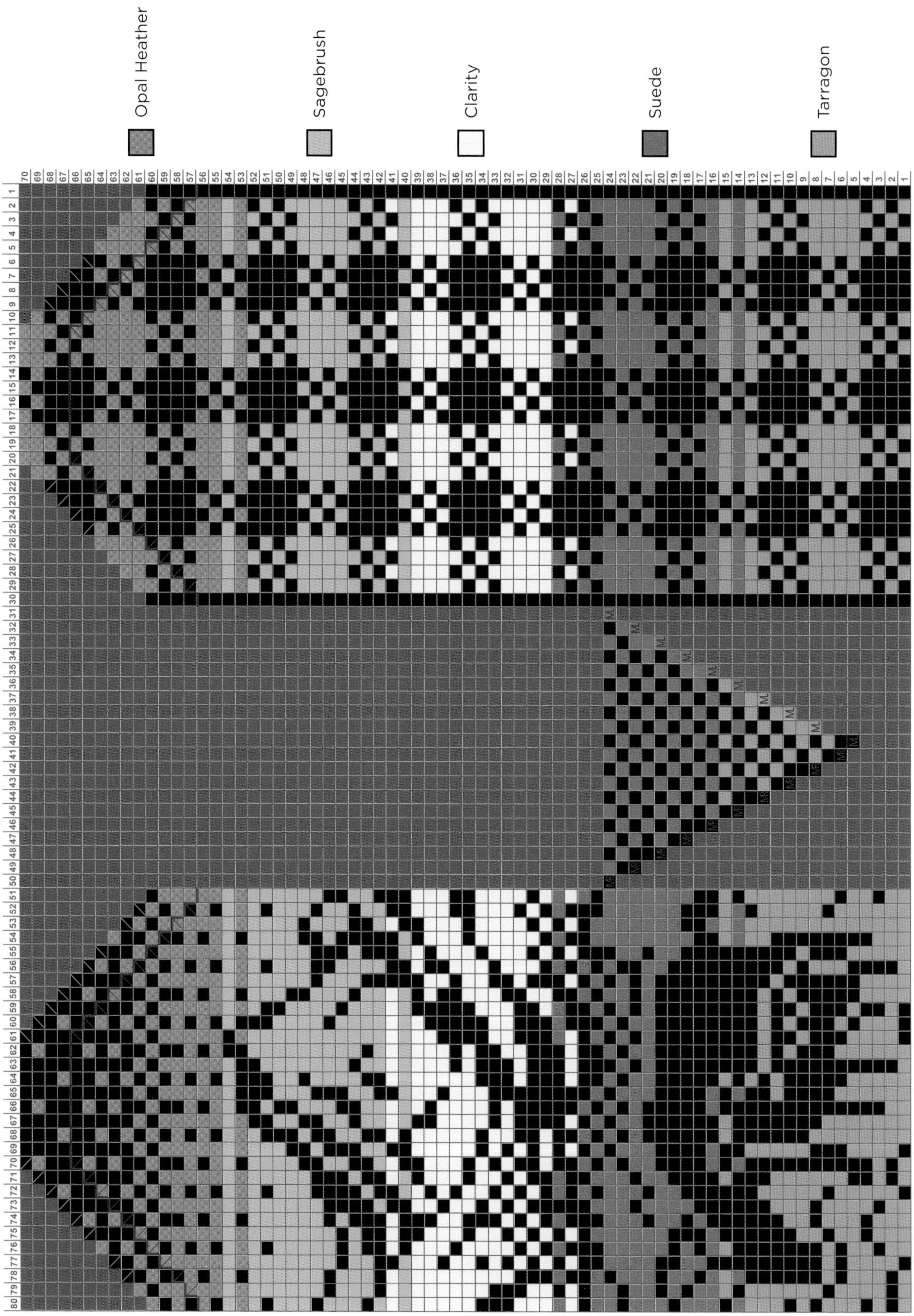

November—Right

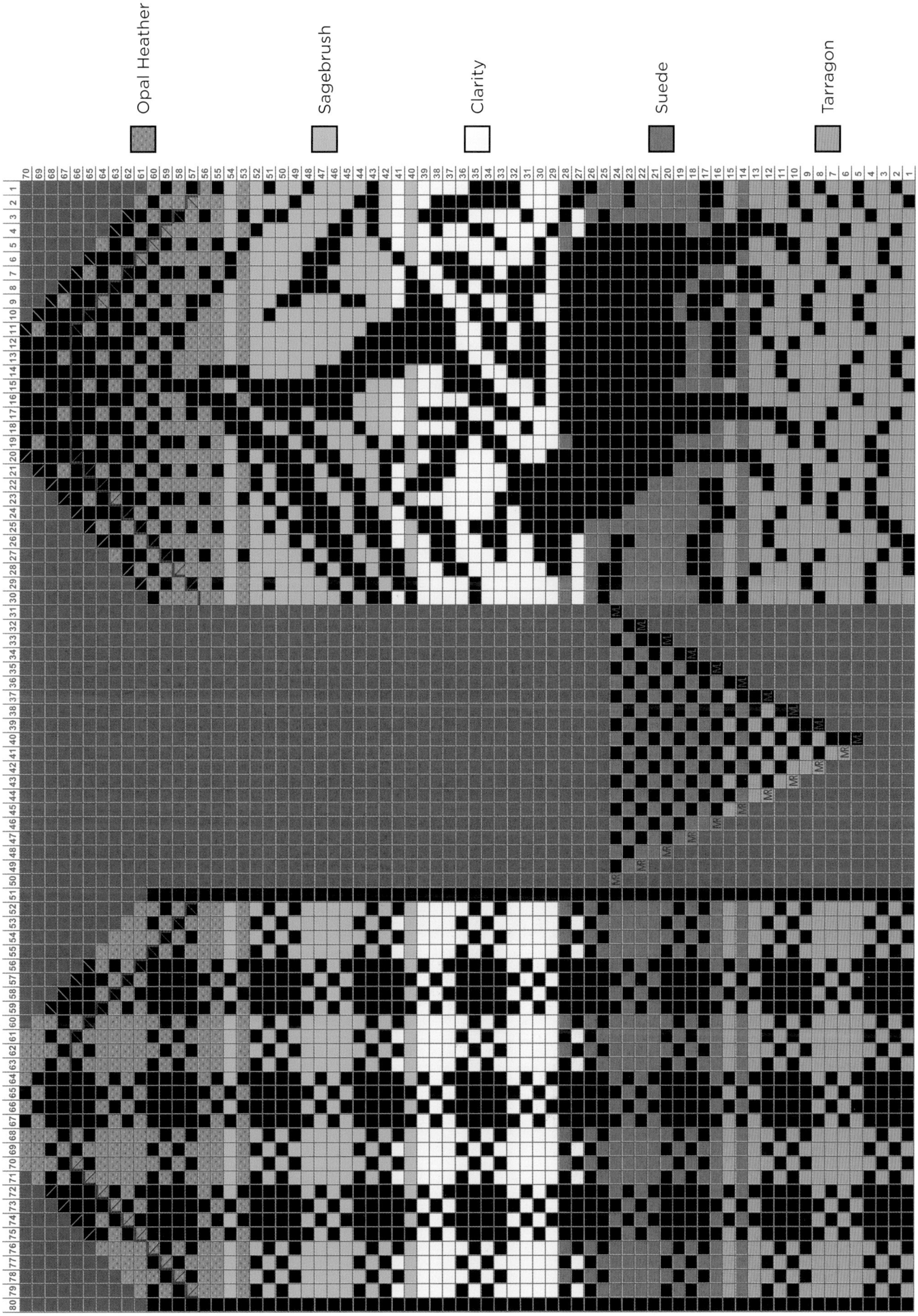

December—Left

- Opal Heather
- Tarragon
- Celadon Heather
- Mist
- Sagebrush
- Clarity

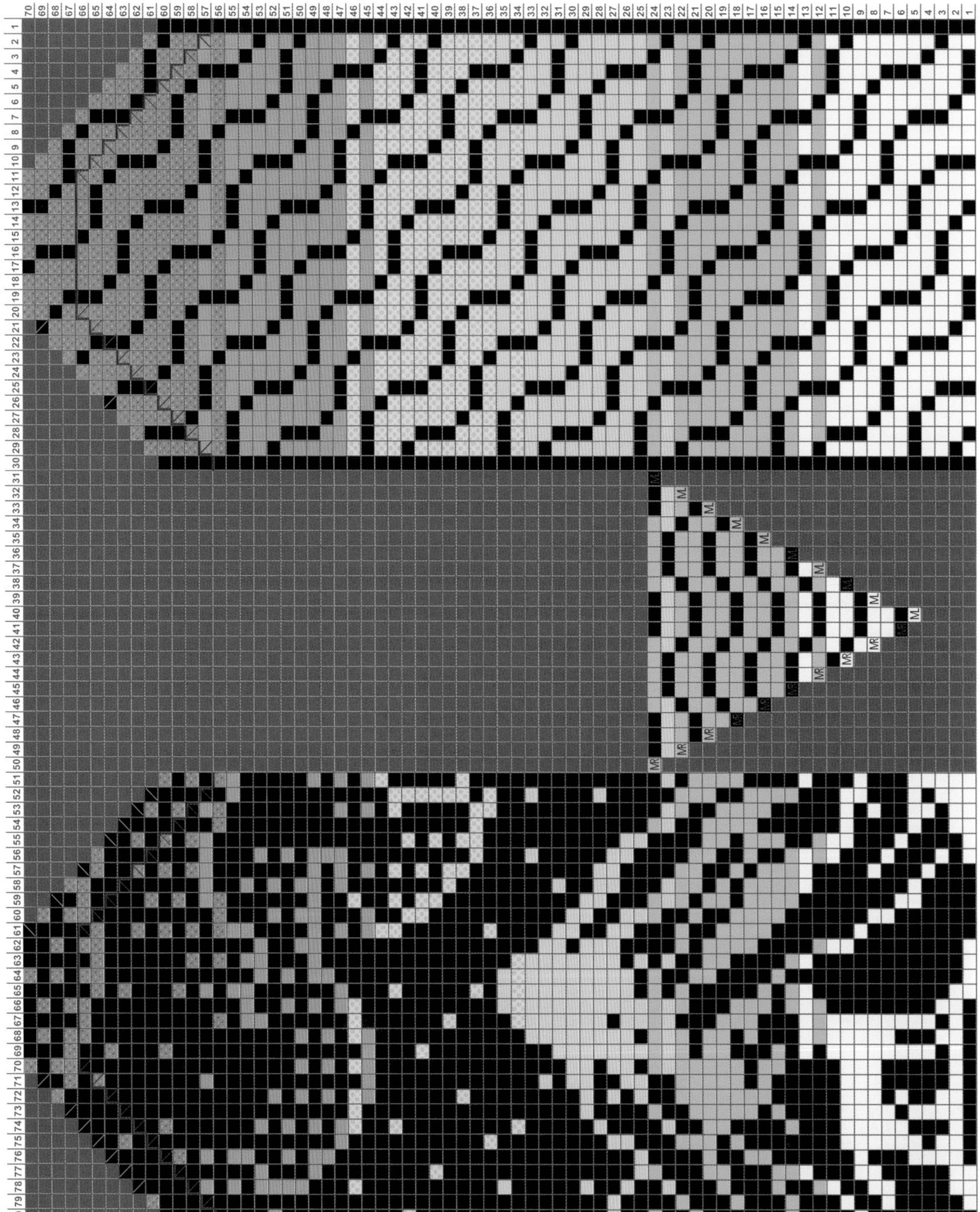

December—Right

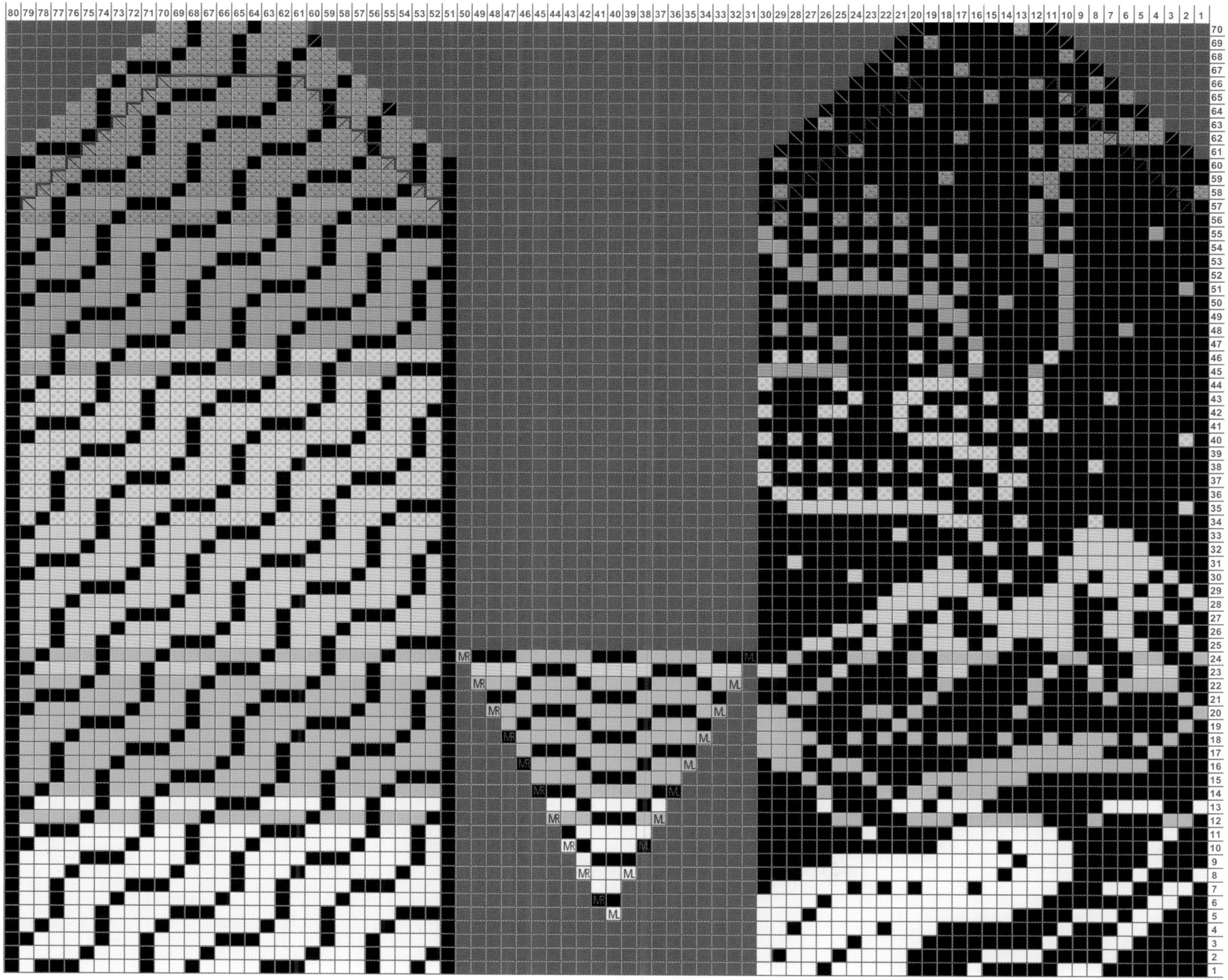

Opal Heather

Tarragon

Celadon Heather

Mist

Sagebrush

Clarity

January—Left

- Clarity
- Sagebrush
- Opal Heather
- Mist
- Opal Heather
- Sagebrush
- Mist

January—Right

February—Left

- Clarity
- Sagebrush
- Opal Heather
- Celadon Heather
- Serpentine
- Mist

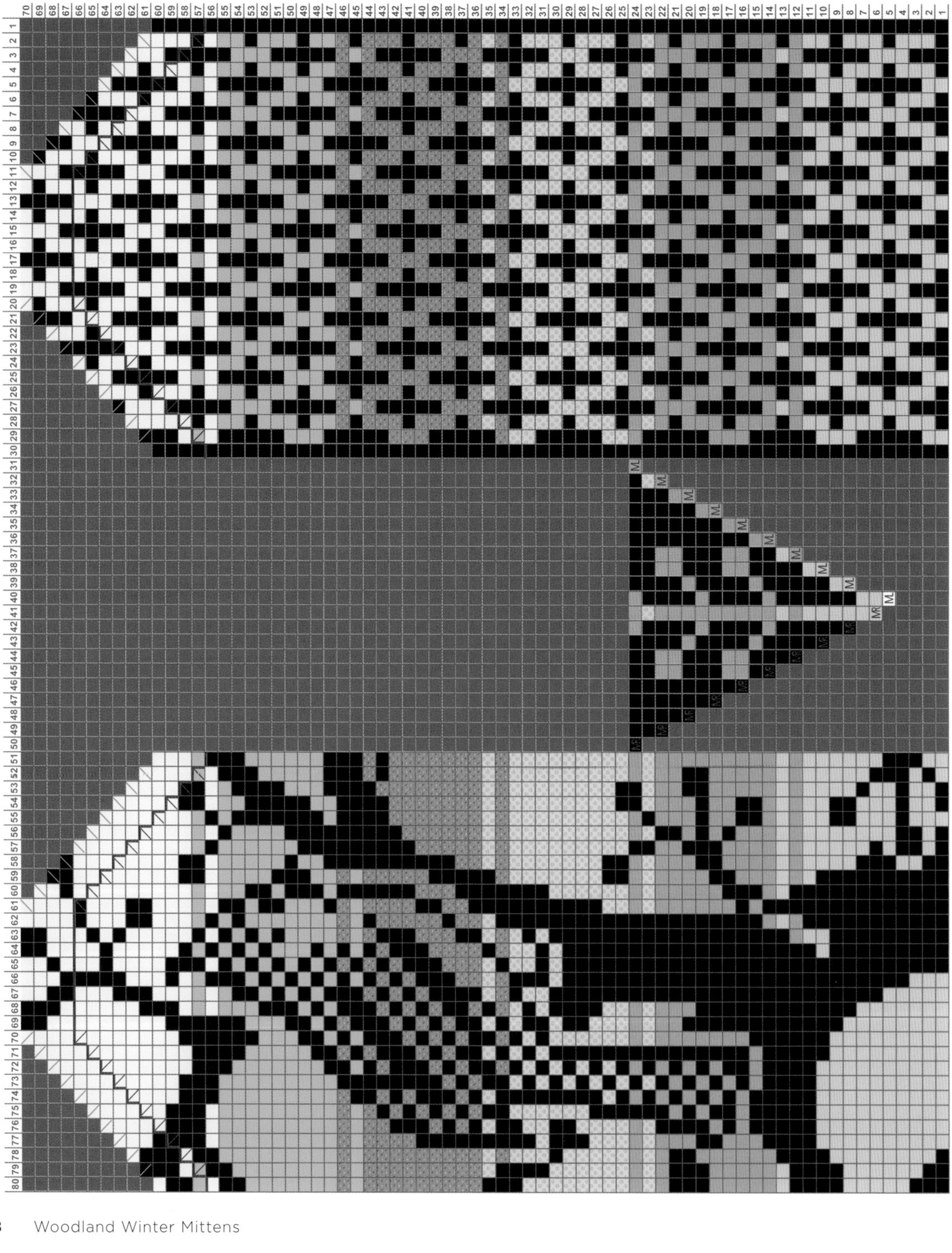

February—Right

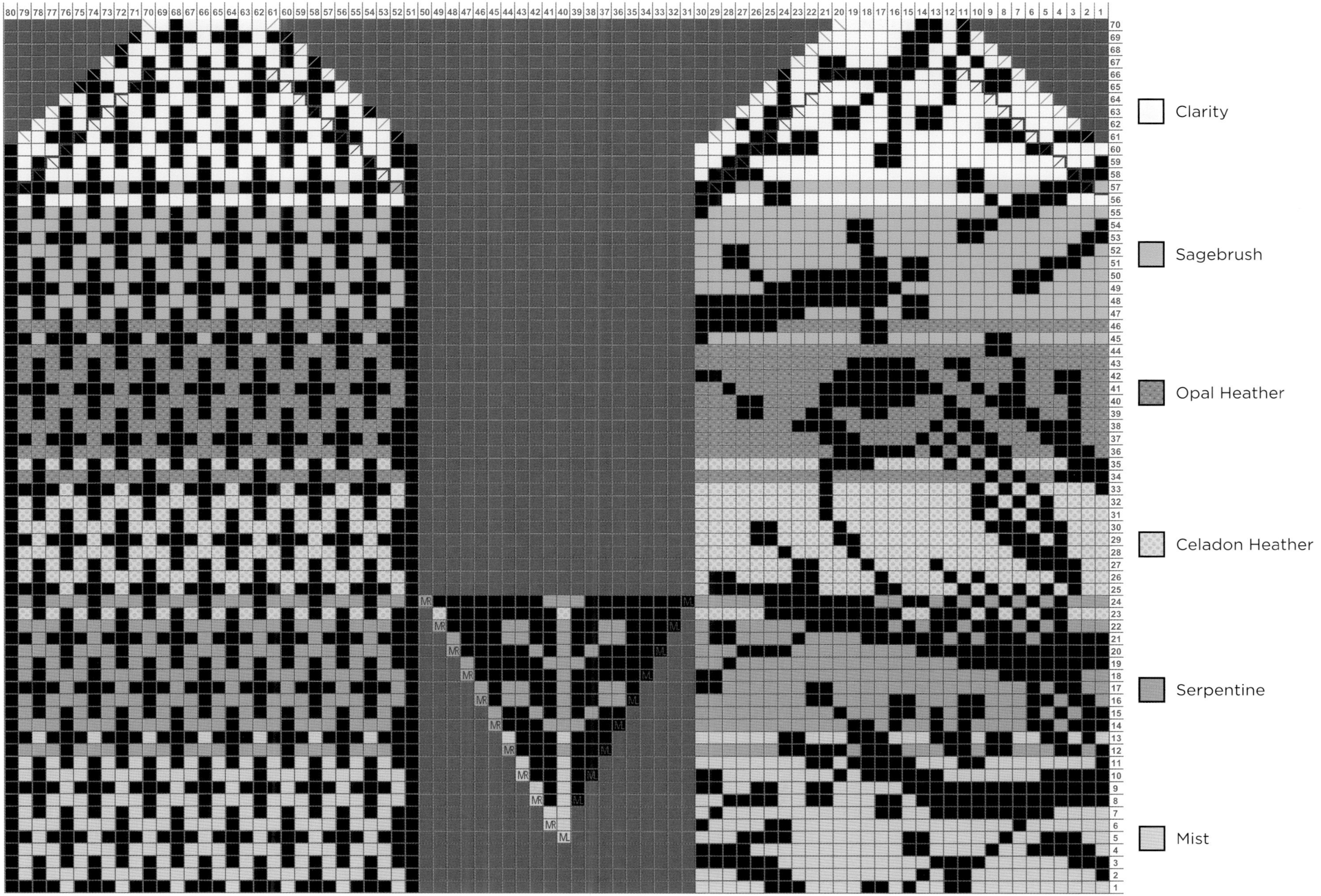

March—Left

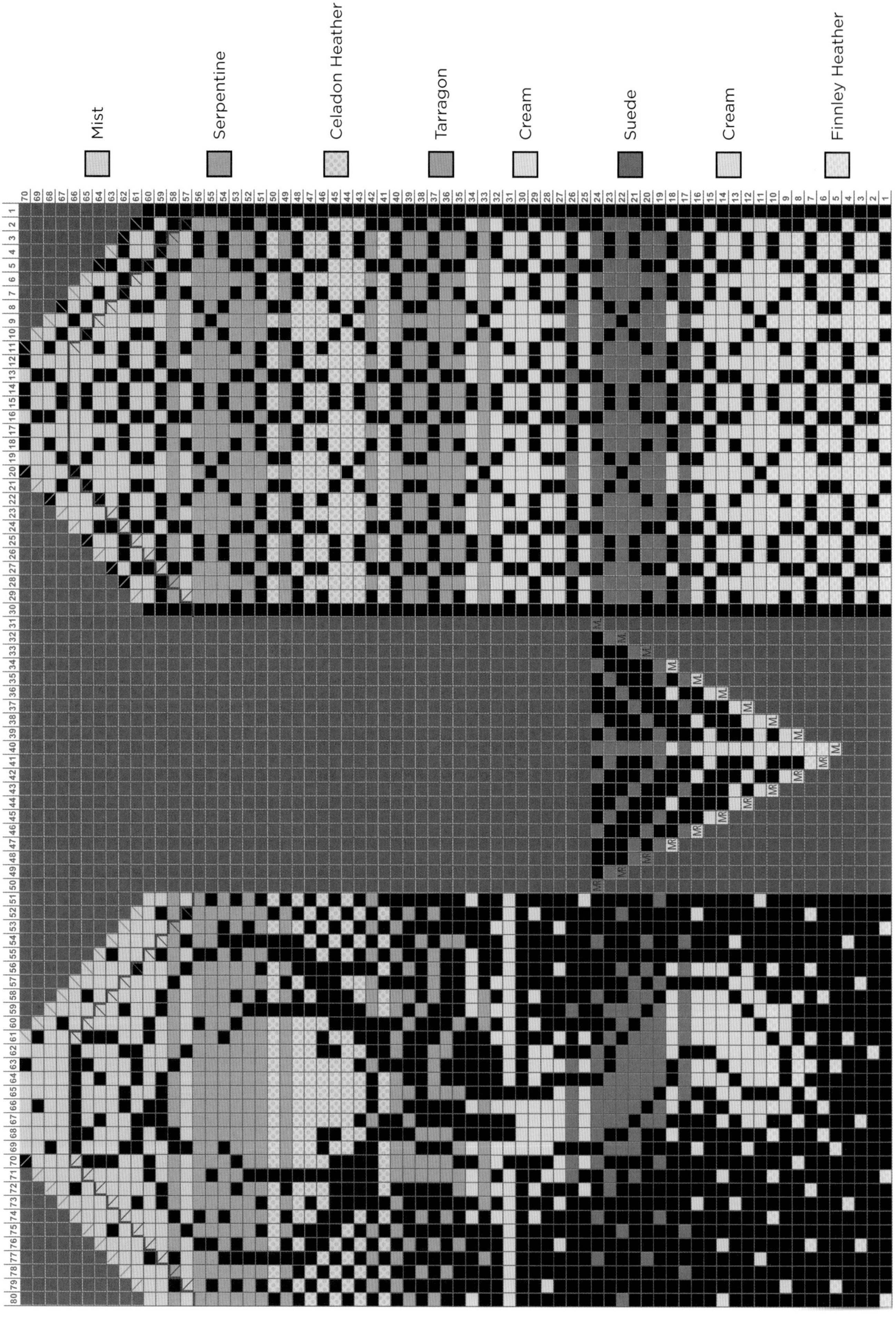

Mist
Serpentine
Celadon Heather
Tarragon
Cream
Suede
Cream
Finnley Heather

March—Right

Mist
Serpentine
Celadon Heather
Tarragon
Cream
Suede
Cream
Finnley Heather

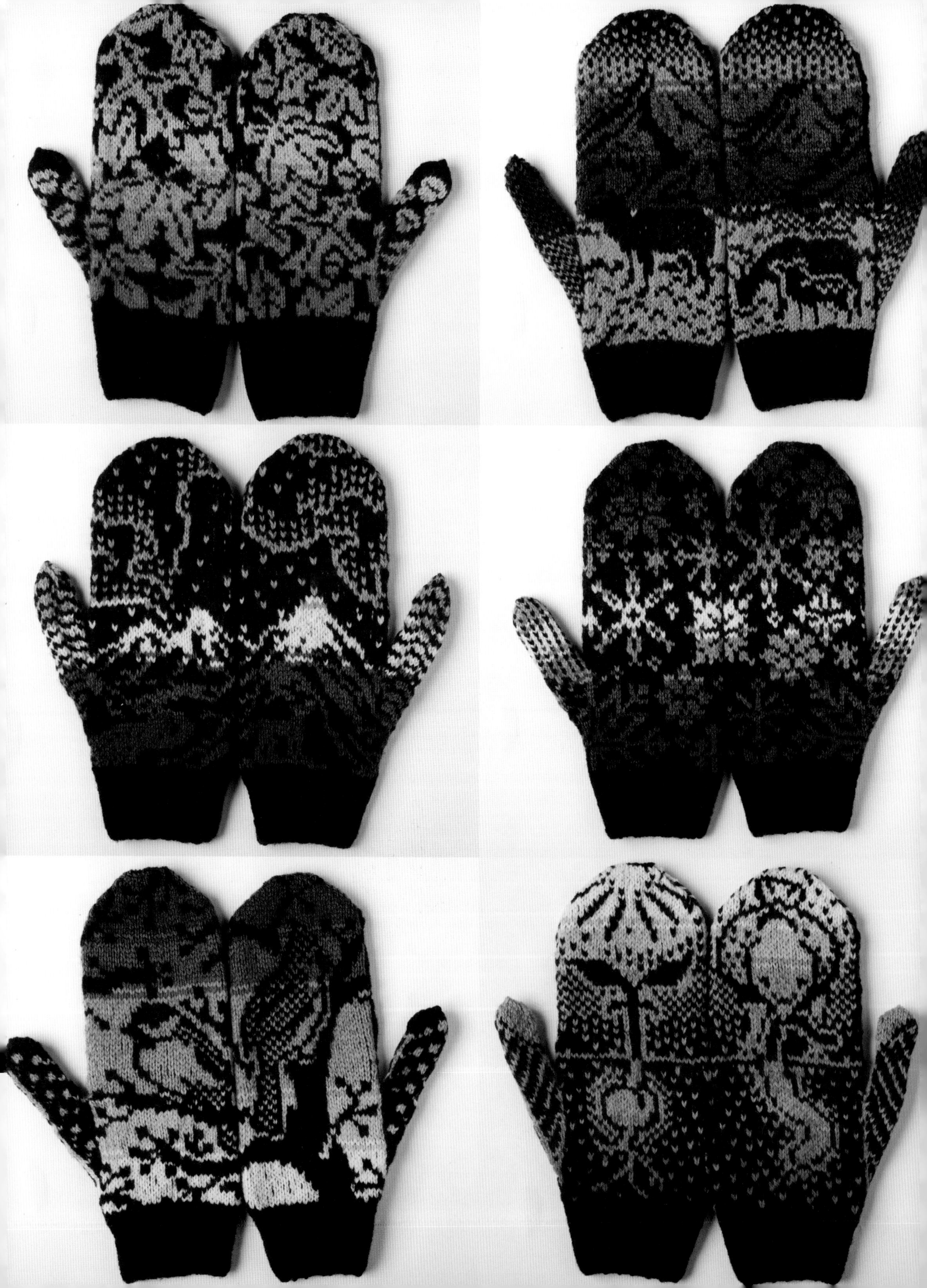

LEGEND: BRIGHT COLORWAY

- French Lavender
- Chicory
- Caribbean
- Tranquil
- Peapod
- Semolina
- White
- Kumquat Heather
- Sweet Potato
- Orange
- Black
- **No Stitch** Placeholder—no stitch made
- **Knit Stitch**
- **M1R** Make 1 right-leaning stitch
- **M1L** Make 1 left-leaning stitch
- **K2tog** Knit 2 stitches together as one stitch
- **SSK** Slip, slip, knit slipped stitches together
- Size S/M Decreases
- Size M/L Decreases

BRIGHT COLORWAY

4 balls:
MC Black 23729

1 ball each:
French Lavender 24575
Chicory 24577
Caribbean 25095
Tranquil 25094
Peapod 25098
Semolina 24250
White 23728
Kumquat Heather 25088
Sweet Potato 24249
Orange 24554

All Thumb Charts

October—Both Hands

November—Right Hand

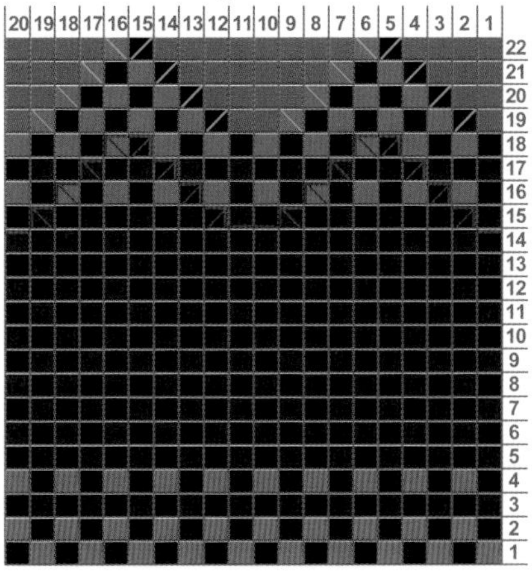

November—Left Hand

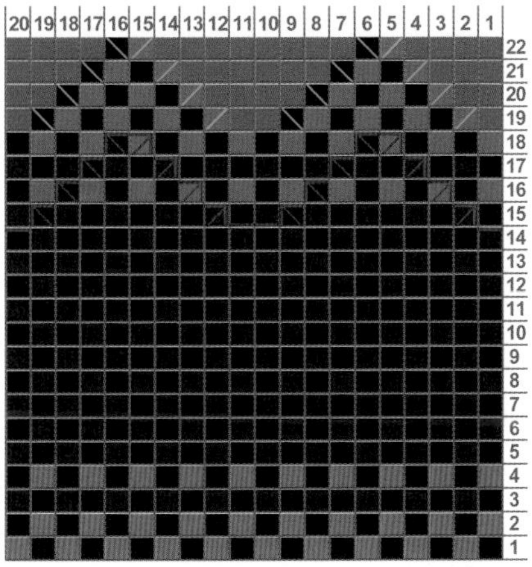

December—Both Hands

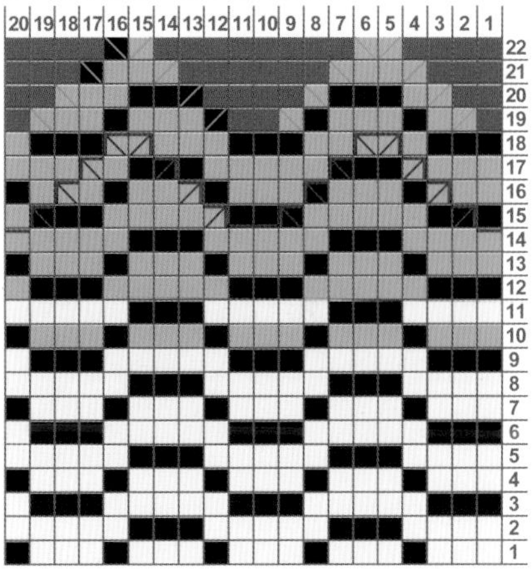

January—Both Hands

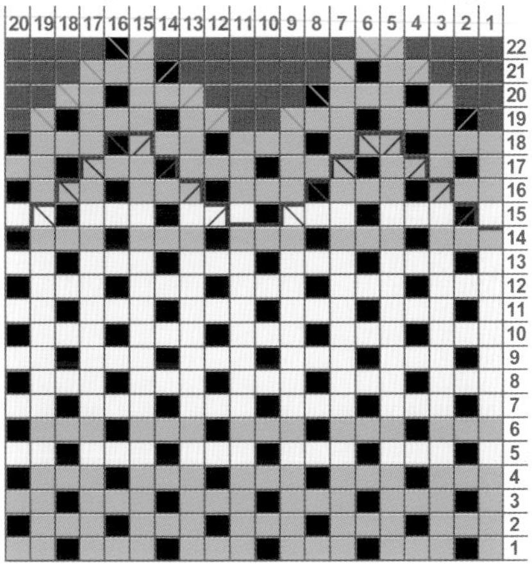

February—Right Hand

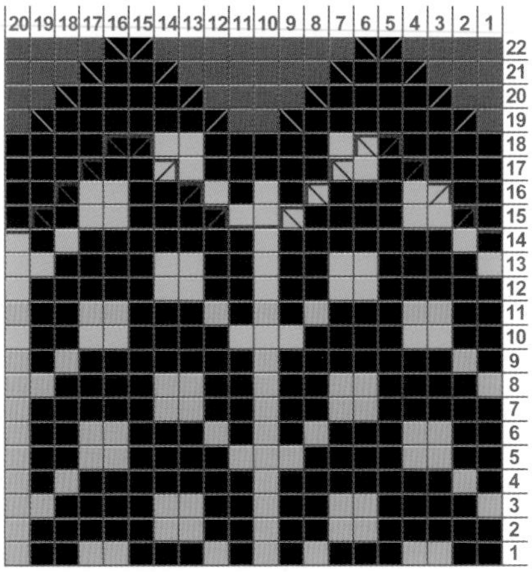

February—Left Hand

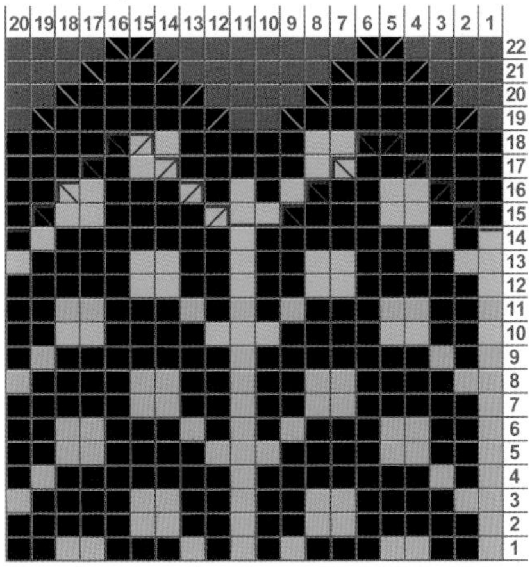

March—Both Hands

October—Left

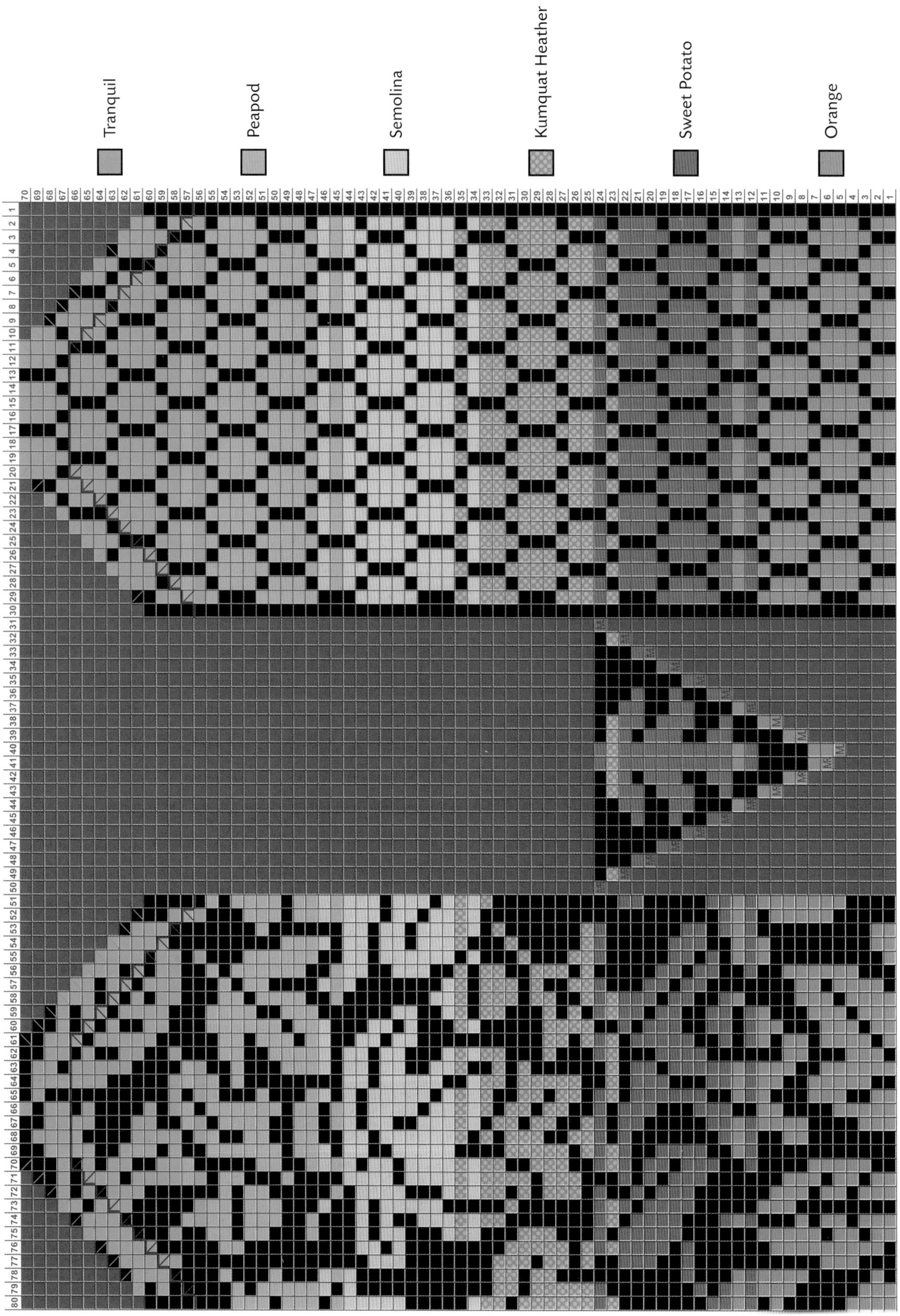

October—Right

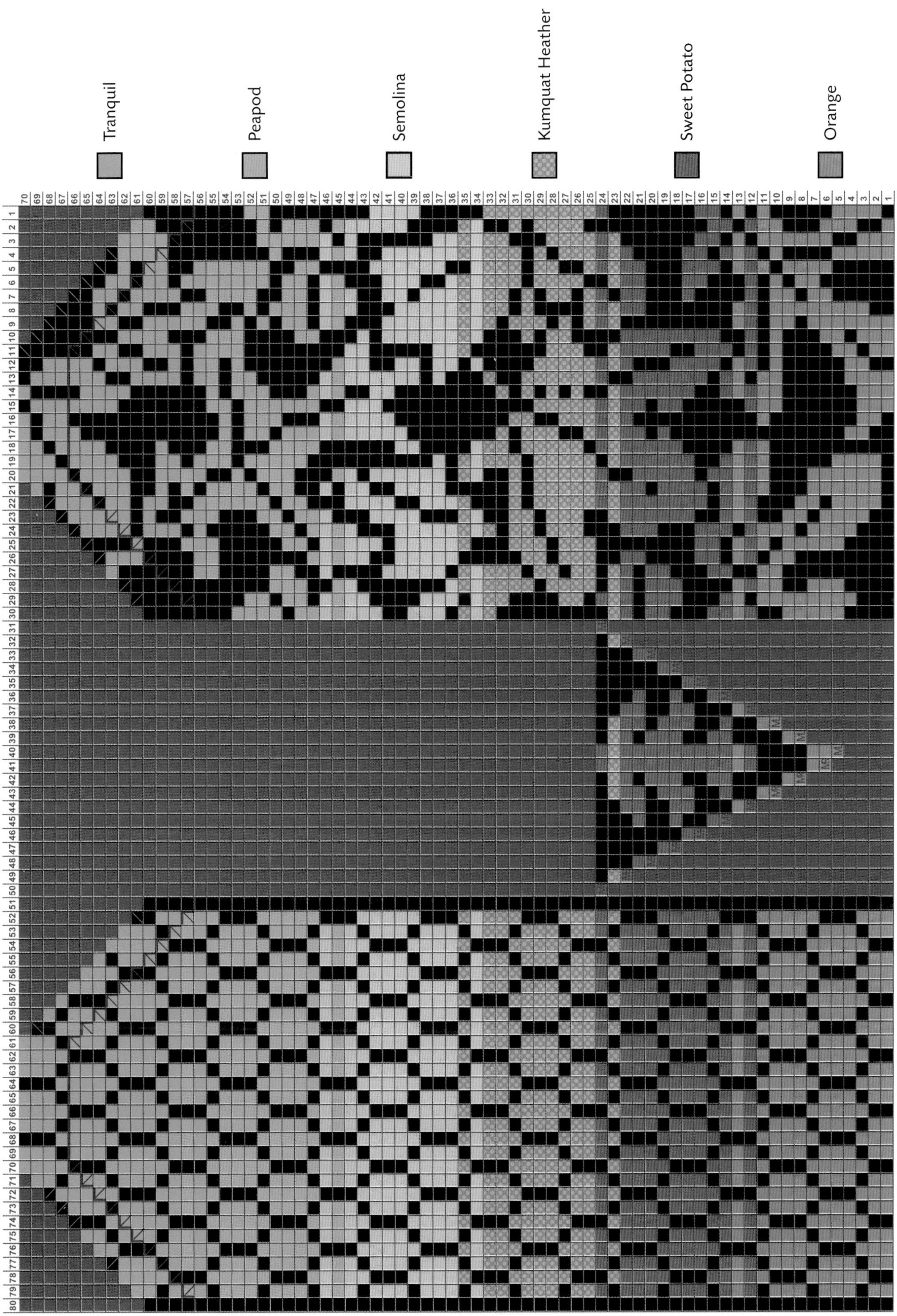

November—Left

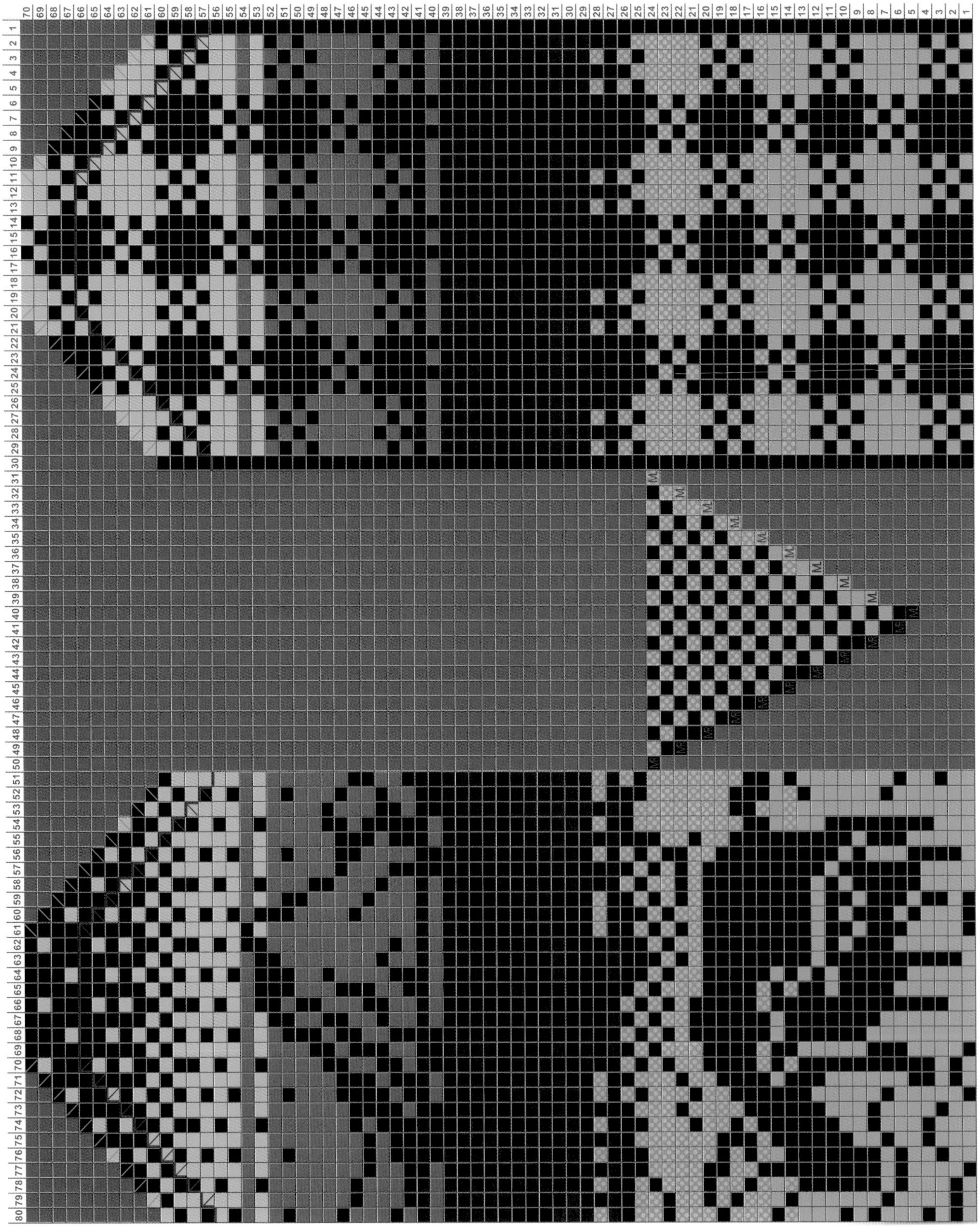

- Caribbean
- Chicory
- French Lavender
- Kumquat Heather
- Tranquil

November—Right

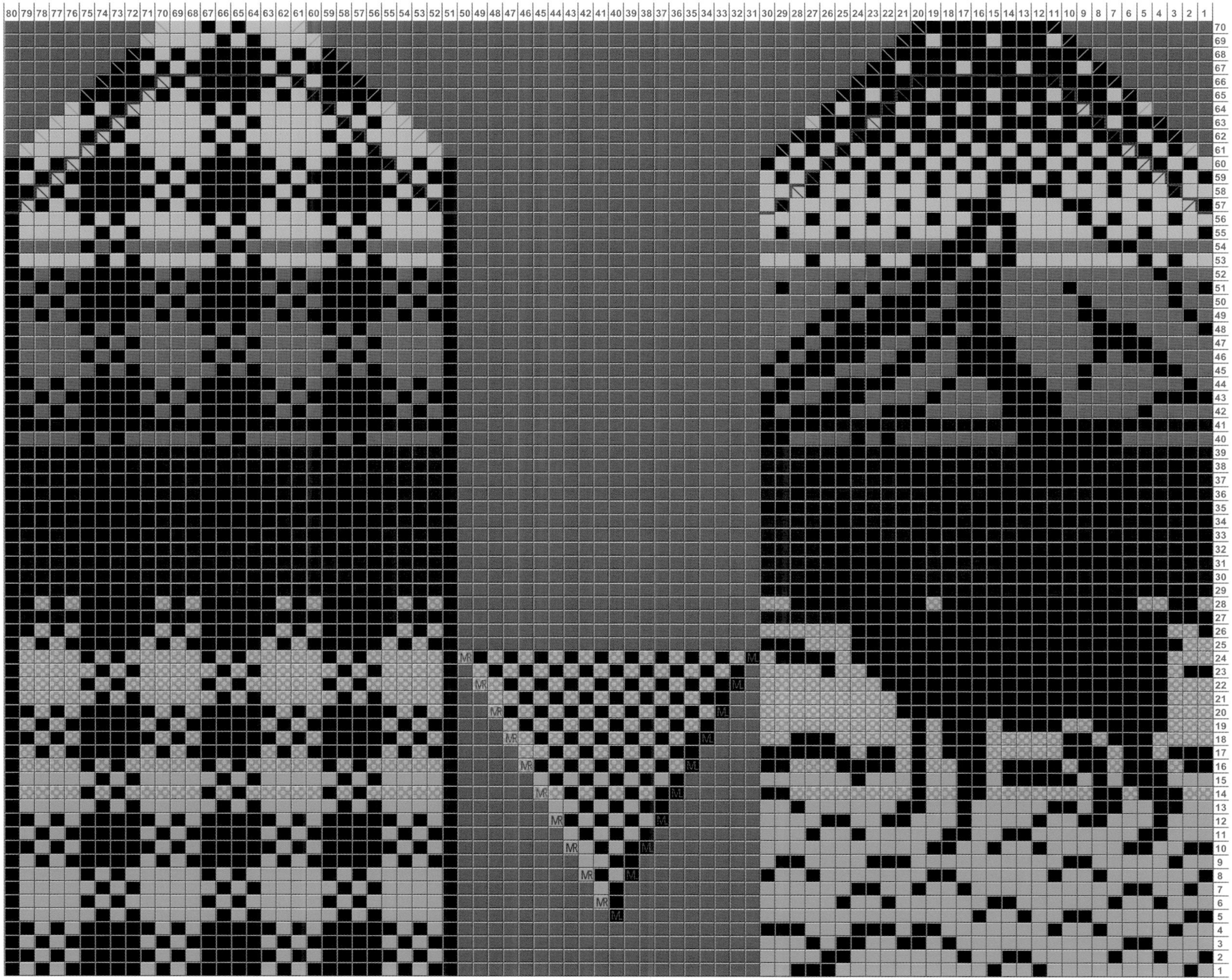

Caribbean

Chicory

French Lavender

Kumquat Heather

Tranquil

December—Left

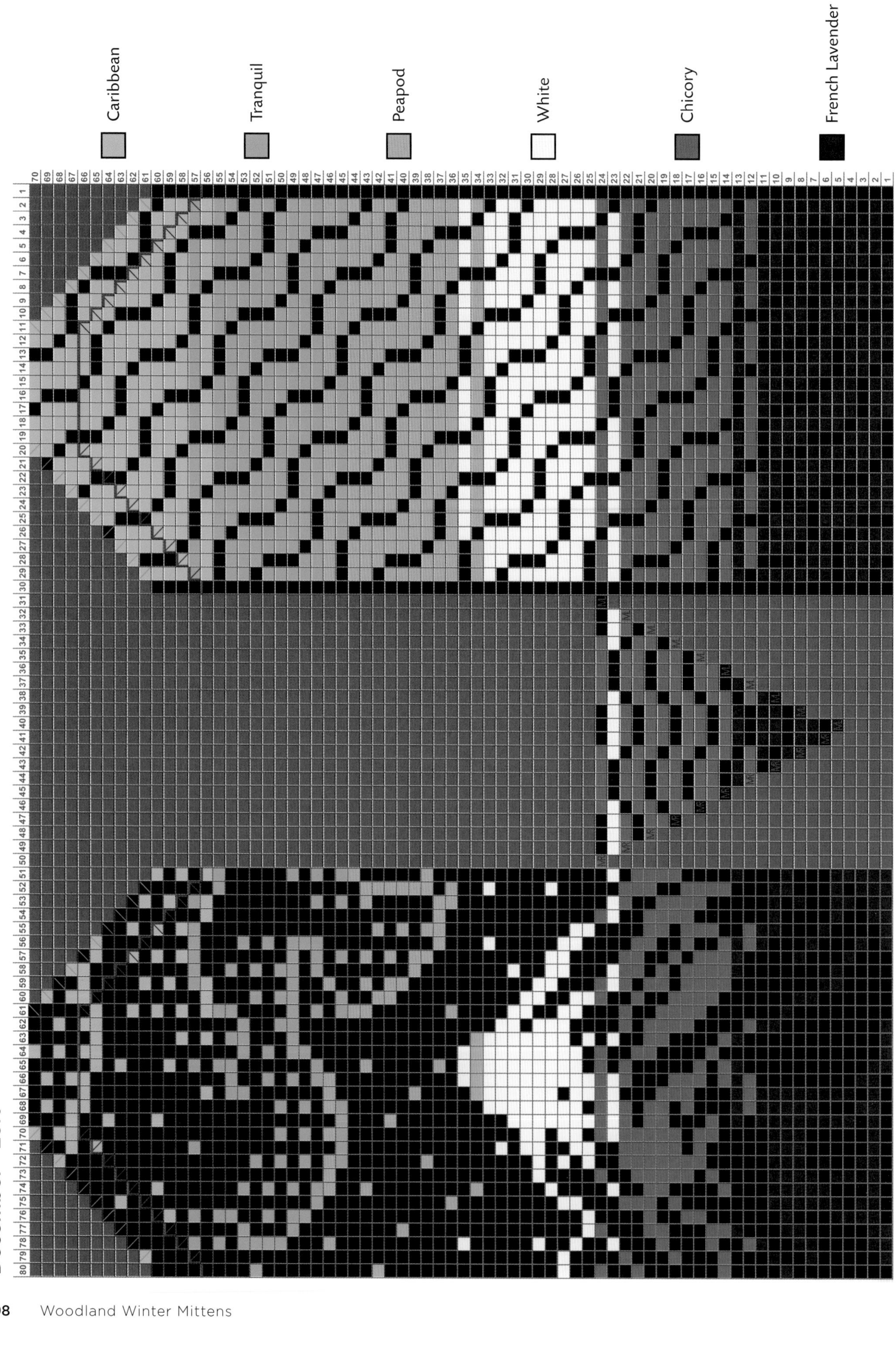

December—Right

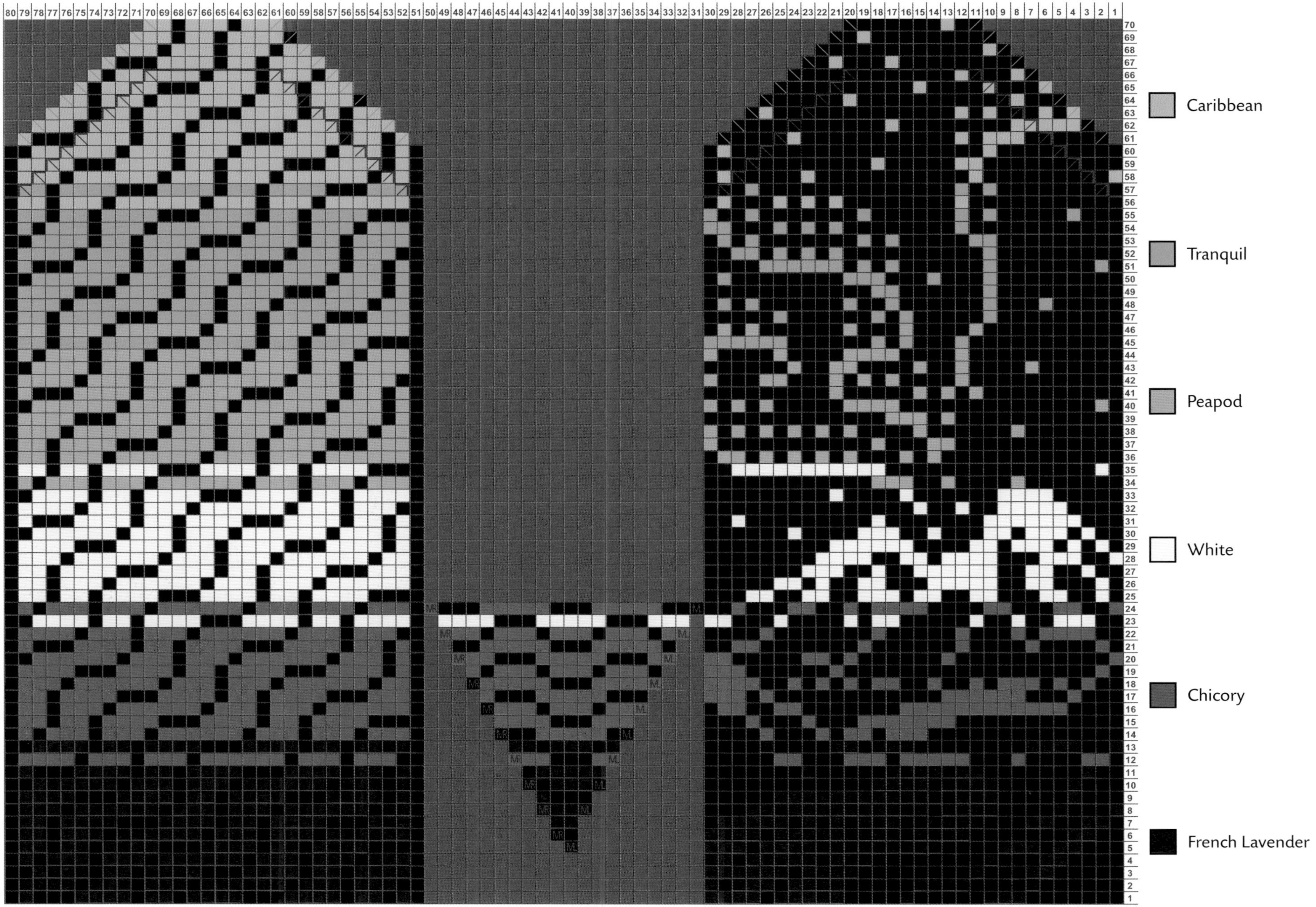

January—Left

French Lavender

Chicory

Caribbean

White

Caribbean

Chicory

French Lavender

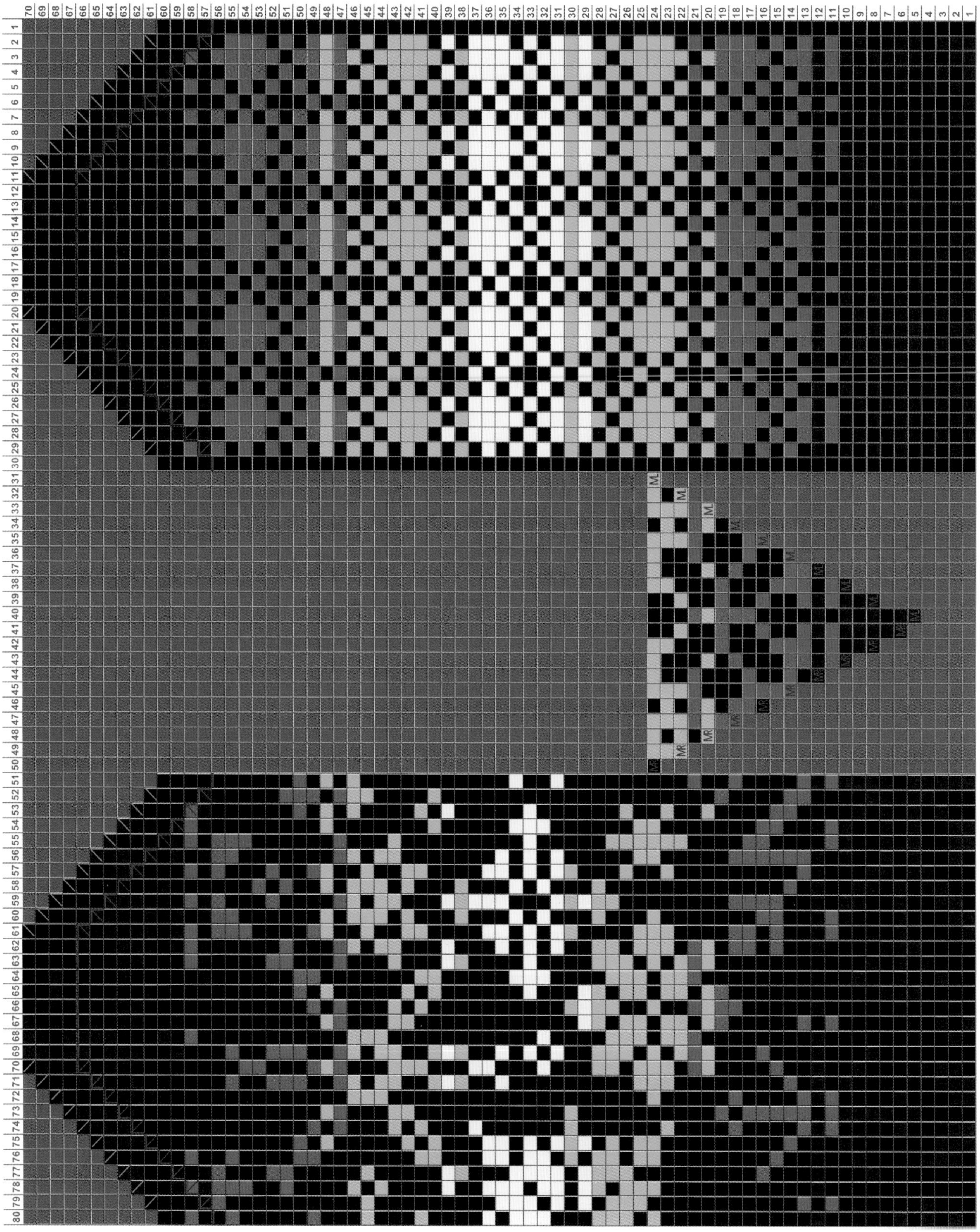

January—Right

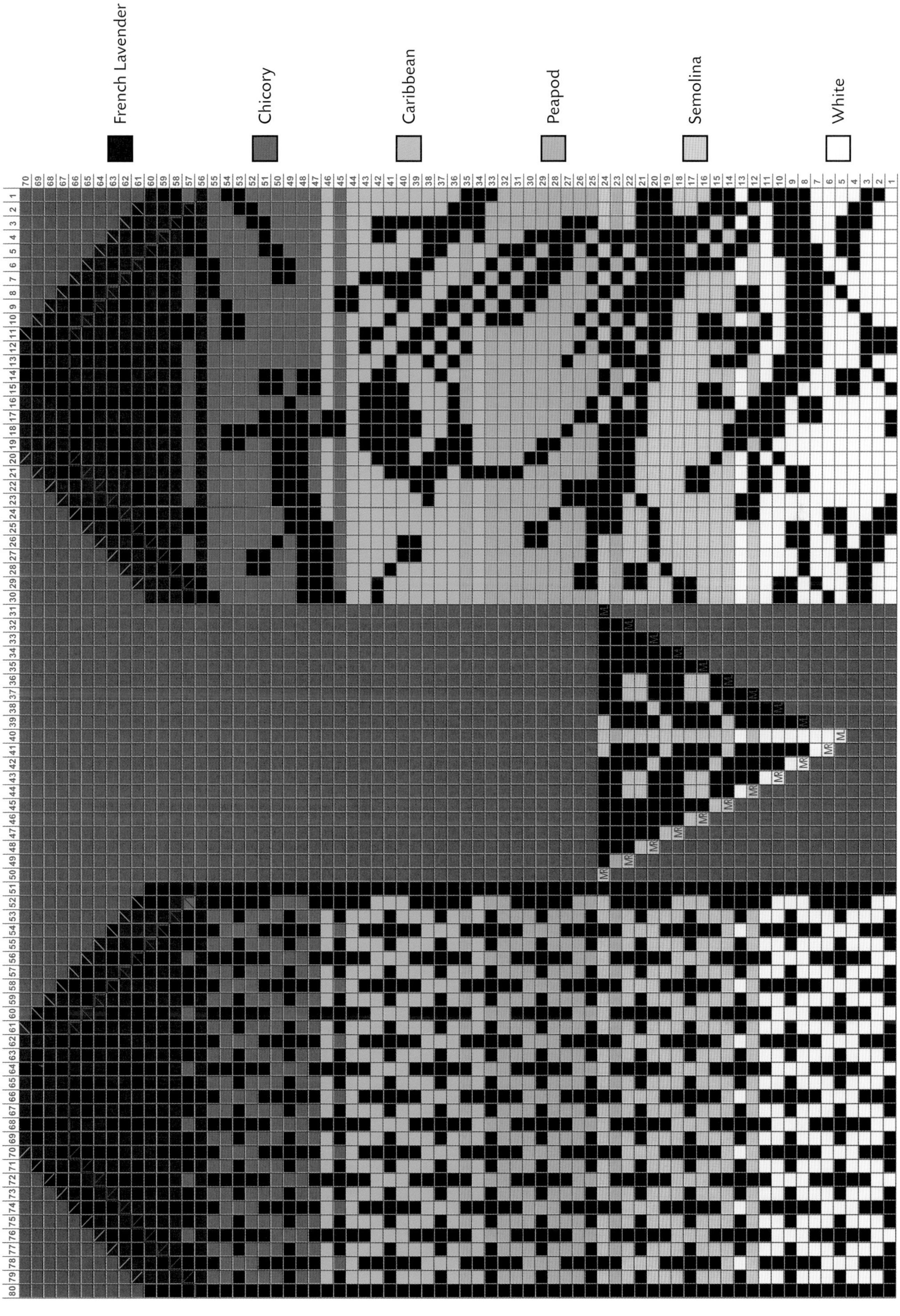

February—Left

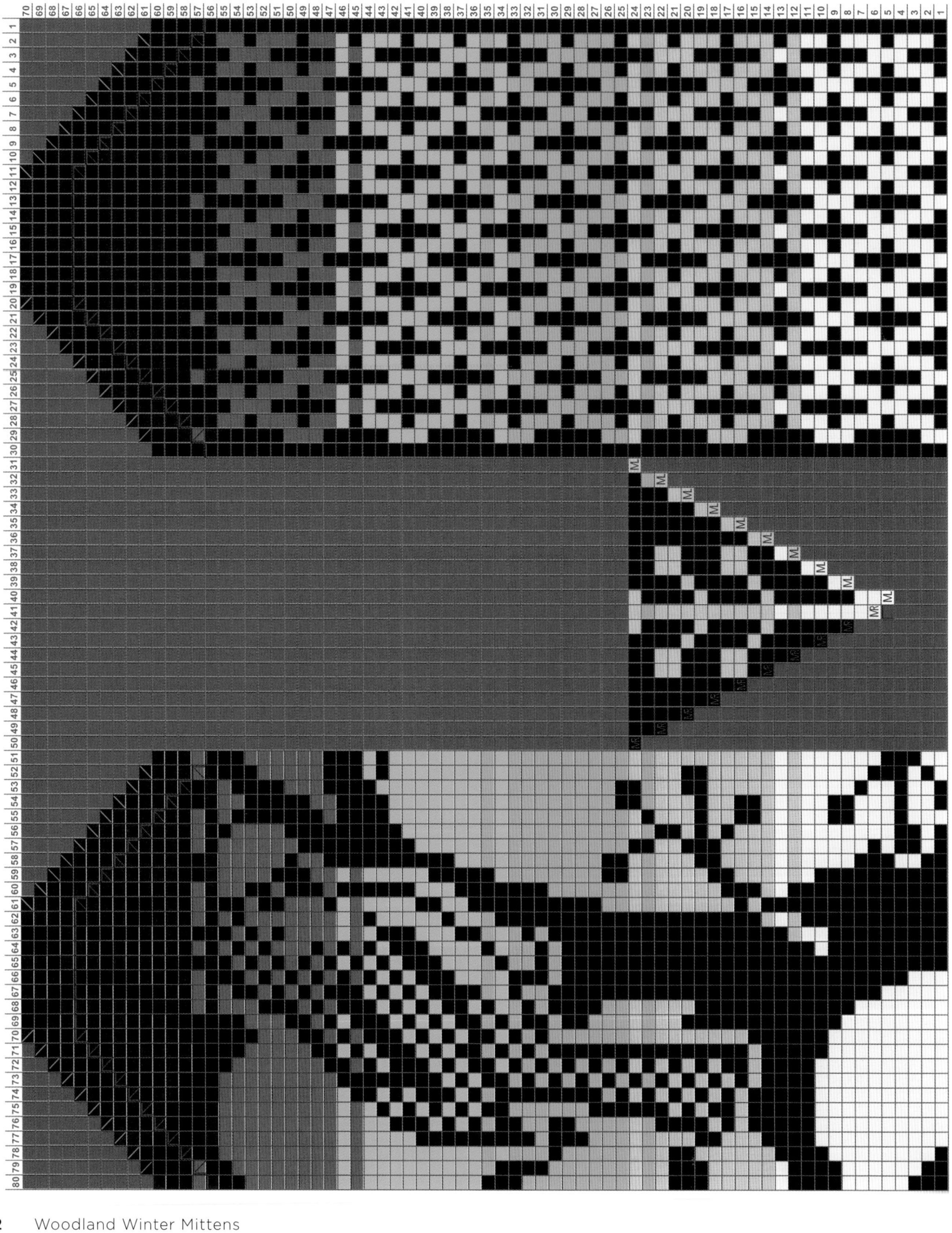

- French Lavender
- Chicory
- Caribbean
- Peapod
- Semolina
- White

February—Right

March—Left

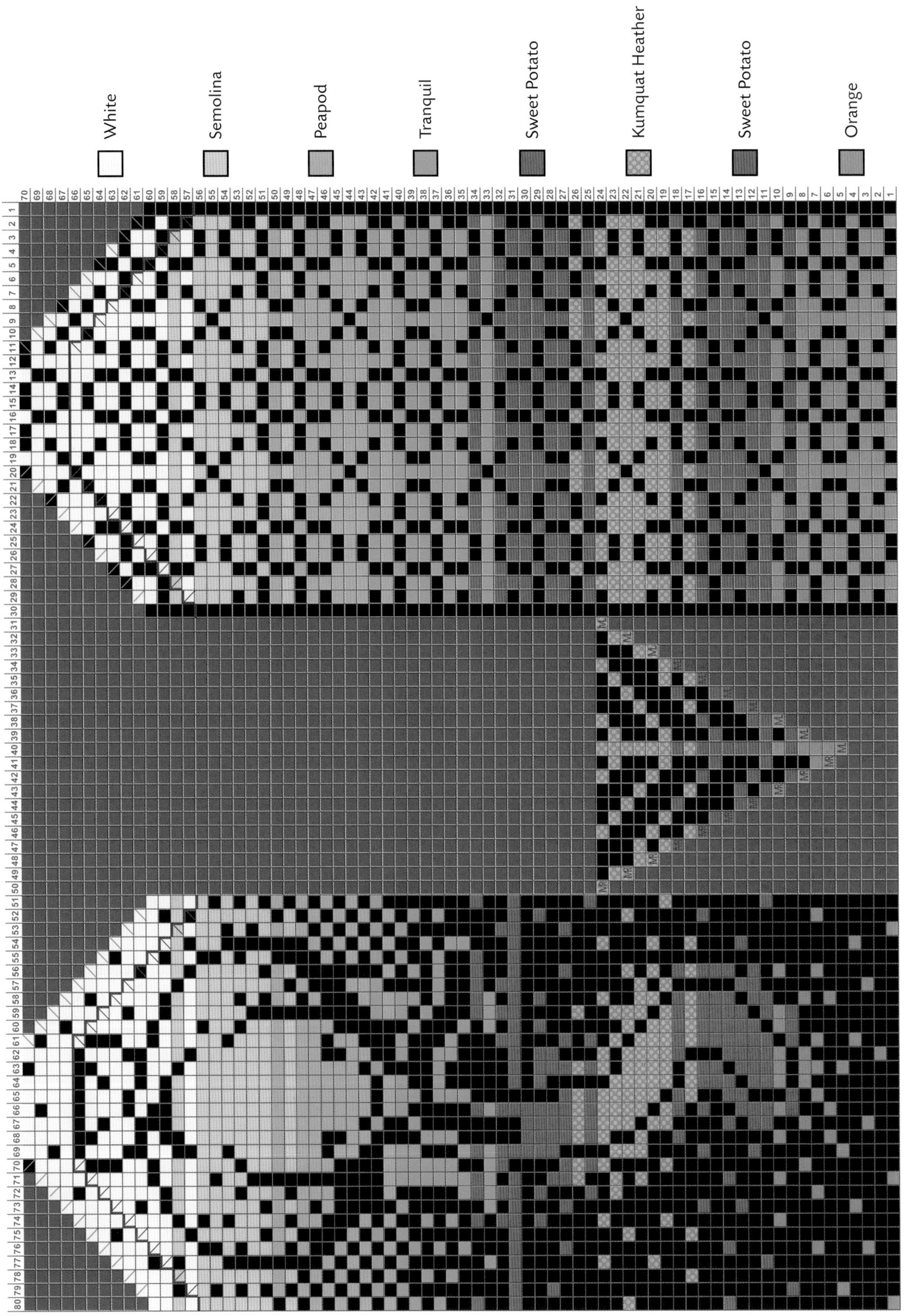
White
Semolina
Peapod
Tranquil
Sweet Potato
Kumquat Heather
Sweet Potato
Orange

March—Right

White

Semolina

Peapod

Tranquil

Sweet Potato

Kumquat Heather

Sweet Potato

Orange

Glossary

Common Stitches & Techniques

Slipped Stitches (Sl)
Always slip stitches purl-wise with yarn held to the wrong side of work, unless noted otherwise in the pattern.

Make 1 Left-Leaning Stitch (M1L)
Inserting LH needle from front to back, PU the horizontal strand between the st just worked and the next st, and K TBL.

Make 1 Right-Leaning Stitch (M1R)
Inserting LH needle from back to front, PU the horizontal strand between the st just worked and the next st, and K TFL.

Slip, Slip, Knit (SSK)
(Sl1 K-wise) twice; insert LH needle into front of these 2 sts and knit them together.

Centered Double Decrease (CDD)
Slip first and second sts together as if to work K2tog; K1; pass 2 slipped sts over the knit st.

Stockinette Stitch (St st, flat over any number of sts)
Row 1 (RS): Knit all sts.
Row 2 (WS): Purl all sts.
Rep Rows 1-2 for pattern.
St st in the round: *Knit every rnd.*

Garter Stitch (in the round over any number of sts)
Rnd 1: Purl all sts.
Rnd 2: Knit all sts.
Rep Rnds 1-2 for pattern.
Garter Stitch flat: *Knit every row.*
(One Garter ridge is comprised of two rows/rnds.)

1x1 Rib (flat or in the round, over an even number of sts)
Row/Rnd 1: (K1, P1) to end of row/rnd.
Rep Row/Rnd 1 for pattern.

2x2 Rib (flat over a multiple of 4 sts plus 2)
Row 1 (RS): K2, (P2, K2) to end of row.
Row 2 (WS): P2, (K2, P2) to end of row.
Rep Rows 1-2 for pattern.

2x2 Rib (in the round over a multiple of 4 sts)
Rnd 1: (K2, P2) to end of rnd.
Rep Rnd 1 for pattern.

Magic Loop Technique
A technique using one long circular needle to knit in the round around a small circumference. A tutorial can be found at https://tutorials.knitpicks.com/wptutorials/magic-loop.

Knitting in the Round with Two Circular Needles
A technique using two long circulars to knit around a small circumference. A tutorial can be found at https://tutorials.knitpicks.com/knitting-in-the-round-with-2-circular-needles.

Backward Loop Cast On
A simple, all-purpose cast on that can be worked mid-row. Also called Loop, Single, or E-Wrap Cast On. A tutorial can be found at https://tutorials.knitpicks.com/loop-cast-on.

Long Tail Cast On
Fast and neat once you get the hang of it. Also referred to as the Slingshot Cast On. A tutorial can be found at https://tutorials.knitpicks.com/long-tail-cast-on.

Cabled Cast On
A strong and nice looking basic cast on that can be worked mid-project. A tutorial can be found at https://tutorials.knitpicks.com/cabled-cast-on.

3-Needle Bind Off
Used to easily seam two rows of live stitches together. A tutorial can be found at https://tutorials.knitpicks.com/3-needle-bind-off.

Abbreviations

approx	approximately
BO	bind off
BOR	beginning of round
CN	cable needle
C (1, 2...)	color (1, 2...)
CC	contrast color
CDD	centered double decrease (*see above*)
CO	cast on
cont	continue
dec(s)	decrease(es)
DPN(s)	double pointed needle(s)
inc(s)	increase(s)
K	knit
K2tog	knit 2 stitches together
K3tog	knit 3 stitches together
KFB	knit into front and back of stitch
K-wise	knit-wise
LH	left hand
M	marker
M1	make 1 stitch
M1L	make 1 left-leaning stitch (*see above*)
M1R	make 1 right-leaning stitch (*see above*)
MC	main color
P	purl
P2tog	purl 2 stitches together
P3tog	purl 3 stitches together
PM	place marker
PFB	purl into front and back of stitch
PSSO	pass slipped stitch over
PU	pick up
P-wise	purl-wise
rep	repeat
Rev St st	reverse stockinette stitch
RH	right hand
rnd(s)	round(s)
RS	right side
Sk	skip
SK2P	slip 1, knit 2 together, pass slipped stitch over
SKP	slip, knit, pass slipped stitch over
Sl	slip (*see above*)
SM	slip marker
SSK	slip, slip, knit these 2 stitches together (*see above*)
SSP	slip, slip, purl these 2 stitches together through back loop
SSSK	slip, slip, slip, knit these 3 stitches together (like SSK)
St st	stockinette stitch (*see above*)
st(s)	stitch(es)
TBL	through back loop
TFL	through front loop
tog	together
W&T	wrap & turn (for short rows; *see next pg*)
WE	work even
WS	wrong side
WYIB	with yarn in back
WYIF	with yarn in front
YO	yarn over

Cabling Without a Cable Needle
A tutorial can be found at https://tutorials.knitpicks.com/learn-to-cable-without-a-cable-needle.

Felted Join (to splice yarn)
One method for joining a new length of yarn to the end of one that is already being used. A tutorial can be found at https://tutorials.knitpicks.com/felted-join.

Mattress Stitch
A neat, invisible seaming method that uses the bars between the first and second stitches on the edges. A tutorial can be found at https://tutorials.knitpicks.com/mattress-stitch.

Provisional Cast On (crochet method)
Used to cast on stitches that are also a row of live stitches, so they can be put onto a needle and used later.
Directions: Using a crochet hook, make a slipknot, then hold knitting needle in left hand, hook in right. With yarn in back of needle, work a chain st by pulling yarn over needle and through chain st. Move yarn back to behind needle, and rep for the number of sts required. Chain a few more sts off the needle, then break yarn and pull end through last chain. (CO sts may be incorrectly mounted; if so, work into backs of these sts.) To unravel later (when sts need to be picked up), pull chain end out; chain should unravel, leaving live sts.
A video tutorial can be found at https://tutorials.knitpicks.com/crocheted-provisional-cast-on.

Provisional Cast On (crochet chain method)
Same result as the crochet method above, but worked differently, so you may prefer one or the other.
Directions: With a crochet hook, use scrap yarn to make a slipknot and chain the number of sts to be cast on, plus a few extra sts. Insert tip of knitting needle into first bump of crochet chain. Wrap project yarn around needle as if to knit, and pull yarn through crochet chain, forming first st. Rep this process until you have cast on the correct number of sts.
To unravel later (when sts need to be picked up), pull chain out, leaving live sts. A photo tutorial can be found at https://tutorials.knitpicks.com/crocheted-provisional-cast-on.

Judy's Magic Cast On
This method creates stitches coming out in opposite directions from a seamless center line, perfect for starting toe-up socks.
Directions: Make a slipknot and place loop around one of the two needles; anchor loop counts as first st. Hold needles tog, with needle that yarn is attached to on top. In other hand, hold yarn so tail goes over index finger and yarn attached to ball goes over thumb. Bring tip of bottom needle over strand of yarn on finger (top strand), around and under yarn and back up, making a loop around needle. Pull loop snug. Bring top needle (with slipknot) over yarn tail on thumb (bottom strand), around and under yarn and back up, making a loop around needle. Pull loop snug. Cont casting on sts until desired number is reached; top yarn strand always wraps around bottom needle, and bottom yarn strand always wraps around top needle. A tutorial can be found at https://tutorials.knitpicks.com/judys-magic-cast-on.

Stretchy Bind Off
Directions: K2, *insert LH needle into front of 2 sts on RH needle and knit them tog—1 st remains on RH needle. K1; rep from * until all sts have been bound off. A tutorial can be found at https://tutorials.knitpicks.com/go-your-own-way-socks-toe-up-part-7-binding-off.

Jeny's Surprisingly Stretchy Bind Off (for 1x1 Rib)
Directions: Reverse YO, K1, pass YO over; *YO, P1, pass YO and previous st over P1; reverse YO, K1, pass YO and previous st over K1; rep from * until 1 st is left, then break working yarn and pull it through final st to complete BO.

Kitchener Stitch (also called Grafting)
Seamlessly join two sets of live stitches together.
Directions: With an equal number of sts on two needles, break yarn leaving a tail approx four times as long as the row of sts, and thread through a blunt yarn needle. Hold needles parallel with WSs facing in and both needles pointing to the right. Perform Step 2 on the first front st, then Step 4 on the first back st, then continue from Step 1, always pulling yarn tightly so the grafted row tension matches the knitted fabric:
Step 1: Pull yarn needle K-wise through front st and drop st from knitting needle.
Step 2: Pull yarn needle P-wise through next front st, leaving st on knitting needle.
Step 3: Pull yarn needle P-wise through first back st and drop st from knitting needle.
Step 4: Pull yarn needle K-wise through next back st, leaving st on knitting needle.
Rep Steps 1-4 until all sts have been grafted together, finishing by working Step 1 through the last remaining front st, then Step 3 through the last remaining back st.
A tutorial can be found at https://tutorials.knitpicks.com/kitchener-stitch.

Short Rows
There are several options for how to handle short rows, so you may see different suggestions/intructions in a pattern.
Wrap and Turn (W&T) (one option for Short Rows)
Work until the st to be wrapped. If knitting: Bring yarn to front, Sl next st P-wise, return yarn to back; turn work, and Sl wrapped st onto RH needle. Cont across row. If purling: Bring yarn to back of work, Sl next st P-wise, return yarn to front; turn work and Sl wrapped st onto RH needle. Cont across row.
Picking up Wraps: Work to wrapped st. If knitting: Insert RH needle under wrap, then through wrapped st K-wise; K st and wrap tog. If purling: Sl wrapped st P-wise onto RH needle, use LH needle to lift wrap and place it onto RH needle; Sl wrap and st back onto LH needle, and P tog.
A tutorial for W&T can be found at https://tutorials.knitpicks.com/short-rows-wrap-and-turn-or-wt.
German Short Rows (another option for Short Rows)
Work to turning point; turn. WYIF, Sl first st P-wise. Bring yarn over back of right needle, pulling firmly to create a "double stitch" on RH needle. If next st is a K st, leave yarn at back; if next st is a P st, bring yarn to front between needles. When it's time to work into double st, knit both strands tog.

Steeking

(Cutting your knitting!)

Hand-Sewn Steek

This technique is useful in those cases where the yarn doesn't readily felt to itself or is at a larger gauge than traditional colorwork. The cut line will be directly in the center of the steek; a line of stitching one stitch to each side of this cut line will help to stabilize the cut edge.

It may help to use a contrasting color of thread; this will not be visible in the finished piece. Once the steek has been cut and the edging knit, a sewn-in piece of grosgrain ribbon can help keep the edges from fraying.

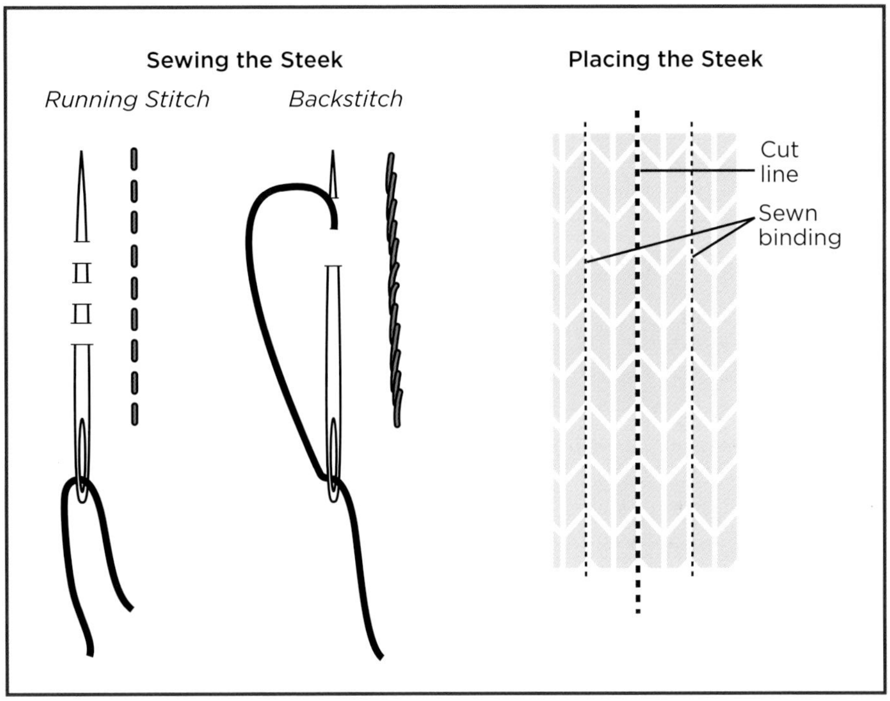

Hand-Sewn Directions:

Hold work so that the steek is in the center of the piece. Reach in and smooth any yarn ends away from these stitches. Lay piece on a flat surface to help with sewing. With sewing needle and thread, sew a running stitch between the first and second stitches to the right of the center cut line. Be sure to catch the floats between every stitch; sew right through the yarn. Turn work and backstitch down the same column of stitches. To backstitch, run the needle under and out as a normal stitch, but begin the next stitch halfway between the beginning and end of the first. This will create little loops of thread in the fabric that can't be pulled out. Be sure to make many tiny stitches and pierce the yarn with each stitch if possible. Do not pull the thread so tight as to pucker the fabric. The more time you take in this step, the stronger the edge will be!

Repeat the sewn line one stitch to the left of the center cut line.

1. Start by bringing a loop from back of work under CO row to front. Leave a 6″ tail.
2. Insert hook between two sts from front to back, grabbing yarn behind work.
3. Pull a loop through knitted fabric and through loop on hook. Cont in this fashion up the work.

Crocheted Steek

A crocheted steek is useful in cases where there is thick fabric. Using a crochet hook appropriate to the weight of the yarn you are using, follow the steps in the diagram to create a crochet chain up the steek.

Crocheted Steek Directions:

Working with the RS facing and yarn held behind work, crochet duplicate stitches between two rows of knit sts, 2 stitches away from the cut line on both sides of the steek. Work 1 crochet loop for every knit row, pulling work tight. Finish by running final loop over the top of the BO row of knitting. To finish, use a tapestry needle to run ends of crocheted chain through the back of itself; be sure to pierce both the back of the crochet sts as well as the knitted sts, being careful not to let it show on the front side.

THIS COLLECTION FEATURES

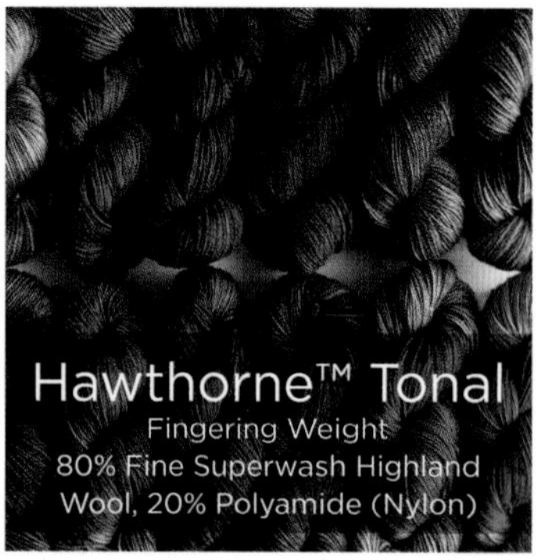

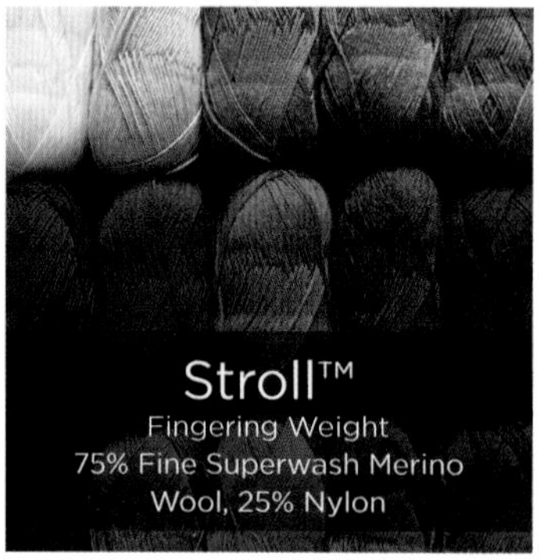

View these beautiful yarns and more at www.KnitPicks.com

Knit Picks yarn is both luxe and affordable—a seeming contradiction trounced! But it's not just about the pretty colors; we also care deeply about fiber quality and fair labor practices, leaving you with a gorgeously reliable product you'll turn to time and time again.